Relationship
Marketing

Marketing in Action Series

Series Editor: Norman Hart

In producing this series, the advice and assistance has been sought of a prestigious editorial panel representing the principal professional bodies, trade associations and business schools.

The Series Editor for the Marketing in Action books is Norman Hart who is a writer of some ten books himself. He currently runs his own marketing consultancy, and is also an international lecturer on marketing, public relations and advertising at conferences and seminars.

Relationship Marketing

**Merlin Stone
& Neil Woodcock**

Series Editor: Norman Hart

KOGAN
PAGE

To Ofra: Thanks for keeping me on the right track, and preventing me from being an even worse workaholic!

Merlin

To Mum, Dad and Julia. Thanks for all the support.

Neil

First published in 1995
Reprinted 1996

Kogan Page Limited
120 Pentonville Road
London N1 9JN

© Merlin Stone and Neil Woodcock, 1995

British Library Cataloguing in Publication Data

A CIP record for this book is available from the British Library.

ISBN 0 7494 1755 2

Typeset by Photoprint, Torquay, Devon
Printed and bound in Great Britain by
Biddles Ltd, Guildford and King's Lynn

Contents

Foreword

Relationship marketing has become something of a buzz-word lately. While the idea itself is simple, making it work in practice is not quite so straightforward. That's why this book has been written. It outlines a complete approach to managing customer relationships, by combining some of the key disciplines of marketing, such as customer service, marketing communications, branding and database marketing.

This book covers the essence of relationship marketing clearly and practically and it will provide useful material for every manager in marketing, sales and service, as well as for senior general management.

At IBM, we have experience of both user and supplier relationship marketing, enabling us to see both sides of the commercial equation. We appreciate the importance of attending to customers' needs, and devote much of our time, resource and technology to managing our relationships with our clients.

I hope you enjoy this book, and find some valuable ideas to help manage your customer relationships.

Larry Hirst
General Manager
IBM Insurance
Europe, Middle East and Africa

Acknowledgments

It's now about twelve years since Mike Wallbridge invited me to help British Telecom (as it then was) move into the (then) esoteric world of database marketing, and Mike and BT continue to influence my thinking. The various worlds in which I have worked – database marketing, customer service, marketing of IT, key account management – have now come together in relationship marketing, so I owe much to clients and friends (the categories aren't mutually exclusive!) from all these worlds.

Of course, it's not just individuals who have influenced me, but also the companies they work for. I've learnt most by working with companies such as Acxiom, Barclays Merchant Services, British Airways, Kodak, Jaeger, Sainsbury's Homebase, Volkswagen, Wiggins Teape and of course my sponsors, IBM, whose ideas on customer management dovetail so closely with mine.

Merlin Stone

There are many people, too many to name, to thank for helping provide the inspiration to enable us to develop the ideas and themes in this book. They know who they are and we thank them.

However, over the last seven years, two people, more than any others, have helped shape and develop my thinking on how customers can be better managed by complex organisations and I would like to single them out for thanks.

The first is Derek Holder, Managing Director of the Institute of Direct Marketing. Apart from his substantial contribution to direct marketing education generally, we have spent many hours together working direct marketing themes and concepts into our overall approach to customer management thinking. For his ideas, support and encouragement, I thank him.

The second is Peter Georgeu, now Managing Director of Direct Access, SA. His undying devotion to organising companies to the benefit of customers, often breaking all the rules and reassembling new ones, has provided controversial and original thinking into the arena of customer management. I look forward to continuing our often heated (but usually enjoyable!) discussions in the future.

Neil Woodcock

Chapter 1

What is Relationship Marketing?

WHAT THIS BOOK IS ABOUT

Relationship marketing is one of the oldest approaches to marketing, yet one of the least understood. In this book, we explain what relationship marketing is and why the concept of relationship marketing has become one of those 'born again' marketing terms to be found on the lips of every marketing manager, most service managers, some advertising managers, and even a few sales managers. We show you how it works and why it works. We also give you the methods and checklists you need to make it work – and to make sure it works.

In this book, we focus on the absolute essentials of relationship marketing. Since relationship marketing is really just a different way of combining existing marketing tools and managing them, we do not cover each of these tools in great depth. Rather, we focus on how you can combine these tools to create, sustain and develop a good marketing and service relationship with your customers. You can find more detail on these tools in the other books in this series.

To help you skim-read chapters, we have indicated the *essential* essentials, the KEY POINTS, in boxed text or in bold text. Also, we have included many checklists, to enable you to analyse your own situation as you read the book.

WHY RELATIONSHIP MARKETING IS IMPORTANT

The reason why relationship marketing is critical is this:

Acquiring customers is much more expensive than keeping them.

This is most obvious in direct marketing, where the costs of acquiring and keeping customers can be accurately quantified. In other marketing environments, estimates show the same.

The benefits of relationship marketing can be shown through accounting techniques which reveal:

❑ Costs of acquiring your customers.
❑ Changes in the number of customers you have.
❑ Changes in what each customer is buying from you.

However, this may mean you have to change your methods of doing marketing calculations. If you quantify markets by volume or value of sales, the connection between relationship marketing and profit may be hard to see.

But if you also quantify markets in terms of:

❑ How many customers you have;
❑ The value of orders each customer places during their 'life' with you,

then the connection becomes clearer.

COSTS AND BENEFITS OF RELATIONSHIP MARKETING

For you, the costs of relationship marketing may be mainly those associated with change and the increased complexity of the business process. Finding out about and then meeting your customers' needs – not just for products and services but also for relationship management – is key to defining these processes. You may need to invest. You may need new computer systems and new procedures. You may need to train your staff differently. Your outlets may need rearranging. Your communica-

You must view relationship marketing as an investment.

tion with customers may change. So you must view relationship marketing as an investment. Your marketing accounting procedures must value the effects of relationship marketing over several years.

The benefits of relationship marketing are usually in one or more of these areas:

---

1. Increased customer retention and loyalty – customers stay with you longer, buy more from you, more often (increased *life time value*).
2. Higher customer profitability, not just because each customer buys more from you, but because of:
   — Lower costs of recruiting customers (and no need to recruit so many if you want to do a steady volume of business).
   — Reduced cost of sales (usually, existing customers are more responsive to your marketing).

THE DEFINITION OF RELATIONSHIP MARKETING

Relationship marketing is becoming one of those fashionable terms that every marketer uses but defines in a different way – or not at all. We define relationship marketing like this:

Relationship marketing is the use of a wide range of marketing, sales, communication and customer care techniques and processes to:

1. Identify your named individual customers.
2. Create a relationship between your company and these customers – a relationship that stretches over many transactions.
3. Manage that relationship to the benefit of your customers and your company.

This definition, while technically a good one, is a little lacking in feeling. In marketing, one of the best ways to define a concept or technique is in terms of what you want your customers to think or feel as a result of you using it, one you could even explain to customers. So for your customers, relationship marketing could be described like this:

Relationship marketing is how we:

1. Find you.
2. Get to know you.
3. Keep in touch with you.
4. Try to ensure that you get what you want from us – not just in the product but in every aspect of our dealings with you.
5. Check that you are getting what we promised you.

Subject of course to it being worthwhile to us as well.

RELATIONSHIP MARKETING AND CUSTOMER RELATIONSHIP MANAGEMENT

In this book, we use both these terms. In many contexts, they are almost interchangeable. Sometimes, a company will use 'customer relationship management' because it doesn't want the idea to be too closely associated with the way it uses 'marketing'. In other cases, for example in some public sector organisations, marketing is not a fully accepted discipline, so the term relationship management (applied to clients, taxpayers etc) is preferred. Some argue that relationship marketing focuses on the use of specific marketing techniques, while customer relationship management describes how the entire organisation works with customers. We prefer not to be drawn into this debate, particularly since the practice of relationship marketing or management is evolving quite quickly.

WHAT'S DIFFERENT ABOUT RELATIONSHIP MARKETING?

Reading the above simple definitions of relationship marketing, you might wonder what all the fuss is about. Shouldn't all companies have been practising relationship marketing for years? The answer to this is, perhaps surprisingly, no. There are many marketing situations when relationship marketing is not the right approach. There are also situations where, in an ideal world, you might like to practise relationship marketing, but it simply is not feasible. When you should use relationship marketing is one of the themes that runs throughout this book. The reasons why you might not find it feasible lie in the way marketing as a discipline has evolved to meet changing markets, competition and technology.

Let's have a look at two important areas of marketing – marketing by the big multiple grocery retailers and consumer goods brand management.

Grocery retailing

Retailing is one of the most important and publicly visible areas of marketing. For most consumers, the retail experience may be the aspect of marketing that they are exposed to more often and for longer than any other. Yet the most successful retailers have done well for years without relationship marketing. Their success has been achieved mainly through good (and tough) merchandise buying, setting high quality standards, staff selection and training, display management, and site location and and development. Until recently, at least in the UK, very few grocery food retailers made any attempt to identify their customers by name, let alone manage a relationship with them. A possible exception to this was Marks & Spencer with its card, but this is used mainly for financial services, and only affects how its customers buy its grocery or clothing products through open evenings for card holders and occasional mailshots or statement inserts to promote particular merchandise ranges or mail order.

Of course, in particular stores (up-market fashion retailers for instance), some members of staff know their customers by name, and can relate to them as individuals, giving them advice on what to buy, and helping them with problems. But this is not a central plank of these retailers' marketing platform.

The reason for the absence of relationship marketing in grocery retailing is that, until recently, it was simply not cost-effective to use it as a competitive weapon. Retail margins were tight, and marketing spend was better allocated elsewhere. Nor were the technologies available to enable the customer to be treated as an individual, cost-effectively. This has changed. It is now possible and cost-effective to:

1. Give customers a loyalty card, or similar mechanism, and reward them (albeit on a small scale – given tight retail margins) for their loyalty.
2. Print out a customised set of coupons for each customer, not just according to what they have purchased on that particular visit (which is not full relationship marketing), but according to what they have bought in previous visits, or even according to preferences expressed in a questionnaire.
3. Provide specific incentives to customers who buy branded produce to buy the own label equivalent, which gives the retailer a much higher profit margin.
4. Stock and operate (eg opening hours; staff shifts) individual outlets based on the identified needs of the most loyal customers.

Whether a retailer needs to do this is now more a question of competitive pressures. These pressures are not just from other retailers, but also from branded goods suppliers whose products the retailer stocks but which compete with its higher margin own-label products.

Brand management

Brand management aims to build in customers' minds a set of perceptions and attitudes relating to a product or service, leading to positive buying behaviour. In order to achieve this, brand managers must know who their customers are, what their needs are, how they buy, and so on.

The tools that brand managers use to find out who their customers are and what and how much they buy are market research and retail audits. They influence consumer behaviour through powerful tools, such as advertising, sales promotion, packaging, display, and the like. None of these tools needs in any way to be customised to deal with individual customers. Indeed, over the long run, the brands which sustain their place in the market profitably, eg detergents, confectionery, cosmetics, frozen food, are those which maintain consistently high levels of expenditure on the above tools. These tools have, at least in the past, been proved to be more cost-effective at developing and supporting branding than, for example, direct marketing.

However, direct marketing techniques and technologies have improved to the extent where several major consumer brand suppliers have developed databases of their best customers, and are starting to send them incentives to buy – the beginnings of relationship marketing. In fact, relationship marketing is becoming vital to brand managers conscious of the power of retailers' *own brands* and the vast knowledge of transactional data that retailers can manipulate to switch buyers of branded goods towards their own brands. Fast-moving consumer goods (fmcg) companies are fighting to catch up with other industries like insurance, finance, automotive, and, even, utilities, and integrate the techniques of relationship marketing with their traditional brand-building activities.

THE INCREASING USE OF RELATIONSHIP MARKETING

Our conclusion from these two examples is that in fast-moving consumer goods markets, relationship marketing is just one approach to marketing, but one which happens to be becoming more important. But in other consumer markets, such as do-it-yourself retailing, cars, and financial services, relationship marketing is either already a central discipline, or rapidly becoming so.

In business-to-business markets, relationship marketing has always been at the centre of the stage. Here, the biggest recent changes have been:

❑ The use of information technology to make relationship marketing more effective and efficient.
❑ The introduction of customer care disciplines, helping to co-ordinate the many relationships that some business-to-business suppliers have with their individual customers.

MARKETING MANAGEMENT AND TECHNIQUES

If you have been trained in marketing, or read a number of marketing books, you may have noticed that much marketing training and writing is from a functional point of view. It describes how specific parts of the marketing function can be managed, eg advertising, direct mail, selling, or PR. Or it describes how to develop particular parts of the marketing infrastructure (eg the customer database, market research, using

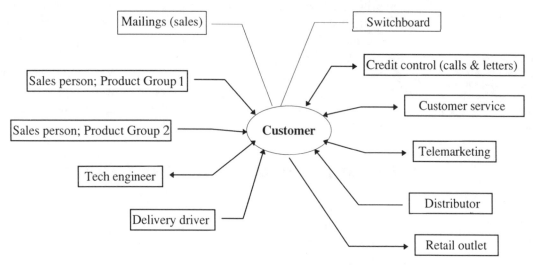

Figure 1.1 Coordinating contacts

advertising agencies). However, from the viewpoint of your customers –
particularly your most important customers, who are usually (but not
always) your most frequent or larger purchasers – all marketing actions
help to create and maintain their relationship with you.

The reason why marketing is usually organised functionally is that
each function uses specific technical disciplines and (often) agencies who
work closely with managers in these disciplines. If these disciplines are
not managed properly, then marketing as a whole is likely to be
ineffective and costly.

However, this 'functionalisation' of marketing has one big disadvantage. It leads to a lack of co-ordination of all the initiatives designed
to influence and manage your customers. This lack of co-ordination is
exacerbated by the fact that other functions, which may not be controlled
by marketing or sales, eg customer service, credit control, distribution,
also have contact with your customers. In addition, third parties working
on your behalf (eg distributors, couriers, transport firms, agencies
handling customer queries) also have their own contacts, as shown in
Figure 1.1.

The result is often that the customer experiences a series of disparate
and often conflicting contacts with you. In many cases, this does not
matter – either because the customer does not expect consistency, or
because the customer derives no particular benefit from co-ordination.
However, in an increasing number of cases, failure to manage the

relationship leads to your customers being dissatisfied, and even leaving you. It can also lead to difficulties in winning new customers because of failure to focus the contacts on 'getting the customer in'.

Relationship marketing provides a framework in which to win, retain, and develop customers.

Relationship marketing provides a framework, within which all other marketing activities can be managed, to win, retain and develop customers. This book lays out this framework for you. It shows you how to identify and analyse customers' relationship needs, and how to meet those needs.

HOW MARKETS EVOLVE TOWARDS RELATIONSHIP MARKETING

The conflict between specialised marketing disciplines and relationship marketing can often be better understood if they are seen in a historical perspective. In many markets, you can see a cycle, which looks something like that depicted in Figure 1.2.

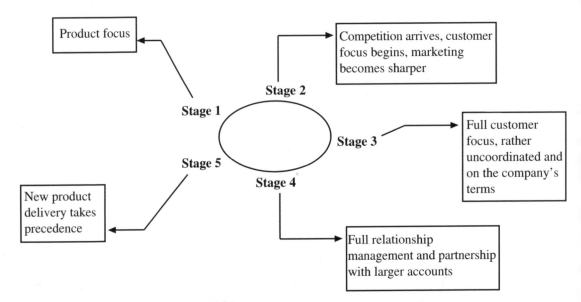

Figure 1.2   Five stages of evolution

We illustrate it using the plain paper photocopier market.

Stage 1: Product is king

In this stage – often an early stage in the evolution of the product – the leading supplier has products or services which are significantly better than those of its competitors, and will gain share and profitability through these products and services. Customers are happy enough to obtain them. No matter how well other companies try to compensate for product or service weaknesses by relationship management, they will lose.

In the early period of the plain paper photocopier market, Xerox's role was once described as 'organising queues for the product'. The service organisation found it hard to keep up with the requirements of a rapidly expanding installed base, and administration of customer accounts was not too hot – although it should have been, as customers were billed monthly, for at this stage the business was rental only. However, the customer base was expanding so fast that customer administration could barely keep up with the workload.

Stage 2: Competition arrives

At this stage, several other companies are producing a similar product or service. Competition intensifies in the areas of features and price. Companies try to maintain differentiation through the feature mix and through branding. In consumer markets, advertising expenditure increases dramatically. At this stage, Xerox still had a lead in product technology – particularly for higher volume, faster machines – but the Japanese were catching up fast. However, in order to cope with the demands of what is an exploding overall market, the Japanese were forced to use dealers to cover the market. The dealers, like Xerox, were very sales- and profits-oriented, and were not too concerned about after-sales service and administration.

Stage 3: The age of customer service and customer care

By this stage, from a technical point of view, there is little to distinguish between products. If companies have been successful in branding (as in many consumer goods markets), leaders continue to lead, and sustain their leadership by high advertising and promotional spend and slight 'tweaks' to the product. But, particularly for products or services where customers continue to use them for some time after the purchase, and perhaps come back to buy add-ons, services and the like from the same supplier, customer service becomes important.

Initially, customer service focuses on such aspects as keeping the product going or making sure that the customer is using the service correctly. But eventually it moves into the area of customer care, the aim of which is to ensure that the benefits the customer derives from the product or service and from its supplier are delivered reliably from the time the customer approaches the supplier. But this is not quite relationship marketing, as the customer who is being well-cared for may still be approached by the same organisation in a different guise, with an attempt to sell the same product!

For Xerox, this was an era when substantial investments were made in customer service systems, service market research, and organising the field service operation to meet not just internal targets (such as response times, ie time the engineer took to get to the customer) but also targets based on what customers wanted (eg uptime, or time for which the machine was running properly). Administration of customer accounts was tightened up. This was the time when Japanese competitors actually took a lead over Xerox in the design of smaller copiers (only Kodak and to a lesser extent IBM ever succeeded in rivalling Xerox's designs for larger copiers), but for many customers, it was only Xerox's service that kept them loyal.

Stage 4: The age of relationship management

With all suppliers having got their houses in order in respect of product, branding, and customer service, at this stage in the cycle companies aim to manage all aspects of their relationship with customers in a co-ordinated way. However, this may not be feasible, especially if companies try to do this with all their customers. So they identify different kinds of relationships which it will be possible to sustain with different types of customers. In Xerox's case, account management techniques were used by the salesforce for managing sales, service and administrative relationships with larger customers, while smaller customers were managed using direct marketing techniques (telephone, mail) with as much automation as possible. The channel management strategy in Figure 1.3 can be applied to many companies right now. It will not be quite as simple as shown, but the result is good coverage of customer base, appropriate cost of contact channel, using the right skill sets at the right time.

Stage 5: Back to the beginning

Some, though not all, markets return to earlier stages. In some cases, radical new product technology can throw the market right back to one in which the product is key and nothing else matters. But once a market has become used to the disciplines of later stages, customers never quite forget the lessons. They will expect reasonable standards of customer

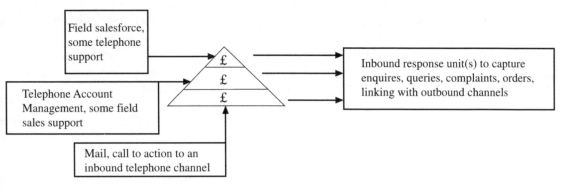

Figure 1.3   Relationship marketing concept: affording market coverage

service and relationship management from new suppliers of new products, even if they are not the best. As soon as competition emerges, they will expect the best. So although Xerox and then Hewlett Packard established dominance in the photocopier-based laser printer market, they had to deliver higher standards of customer service and relationship management than was the case in the early days of photocopiers.

Before embarking on a programme of initiating or improving relationship marketing, it is vital for the company to identify where it stands in this cycle, for this will tell it what its priorities should be.

GAINING A COMPETITIVE EDGE THROUGH RELATIONSHIP MARKETING

The above example shows that the importance of relation- ship marketing depends partly on whether an edge has already been gained by any other players in the market. If not, the potential for increased market share and profit is great. But if one or more of the competitors are already leading on quality, then differentiation is the main option. Relationship marketing is not an option but an essential.

However, in this situation, simple emulation is not a good recipe for success. Differentiation means standing out from the crowd. Some basic customer research will show that there are many things that are quite important to your customers but which your competitors do badly. Today, most, though by no means all, suppliers have improved their performance in areas that matter most to customers. It is in second-order needs that the key to competitiveness may lie, and in ensuring that the best-laid plans are actually delivered: at the point of contact with the customer. Being best at things that other suppliers do badly but which are quite important may be the best route to success.

However, the professionalism with which your relationship marketing is managed (designed, planned and implemented) does offer you scope for differentiation. Positioning is an important part of this too. It supports, and is supported by, good relationship marketing. All aspects of contact with your customers must be managed and presented to them so as to reinforce positioning.

RELATIONSHIP MARKETING AND THE PRODUCT

In competitive markets, a key element in marketing is defining and bringing to the market products which meet customer needs while making the right profit for the supplier. However, usually the customer does not just buy a physical product or a tightly defined service. Customers buy a product, associated services, and indeed the whole relationship with the supplier. Most customers' perceptions of the product are affected by their perceptions of other elements of the package, and vice versa. This is called the 'halo' effect – although in some cases 'horns' might be a better word. Hence the earlier emphasis on consistency of approach.

However, the idea of the product or service coming packaged in a variety of other elements is also a reminder not to ignore what these other elements are. Some may be under your control (eg sales documentation, packaging, telephone hotline), others less so (eg if you are a product manufacturer selling through retailers, the retail situation is not in your control). So it is important to:

❑ Identify all elements of the package which might be perceived by your customers as very important or important.
❑ Seek to optimise them, as far as possible.
❑ Ensure that the plan is being delivered at the point of contact with customers.

WHO OWNS THE CUSTOMER?

This is one of the oldest questions in marketing. Whenever we are asked this question, we refuse to answer it, because it is the wrong question!

The only correct answer is, of course, that your customers do. The question is usually better phrased as:

'Which department, function or individual inside your company has the right to determine how contacts with customers should be managed?'

The answer to this is in two parts. If you have no relationship marketing policy, then it is likely that at the moment *every* department, function or individual in contact with your customers feels that they have the right to control the relationship, or at least their part of it. Because no-one has worked out the commercial consequences of this – in the hard language of losses caused by messing your customers up, confusing them or failing to meet their needs – it is all too easy to accept the *status quo*.

Our answer is that *you* can only answer this question as part of a process, which includes:

1. identifying and analysing *your* customers' specific relationship needs;
2. planning how you are to meet them;
3. establishing a process and organisation for so doing;
4. monitoring that process in action.

Where your relationship with customers is shared with third parties, the answer will depend on the relationship between those third parties and you. Motor manufacturers, for example, selling through dealers, control more of the relationship than, say, grocery food manufacturers selling through retailers. In most cases, there is implicit or explicit agreement about 'terms of engagement' – what the different partners in the supply chain can and can't do with customers, and who gets paid for what. But if your arrangements depart too far from what customers want – and your competitors don't allow this to happen – then you and your business partners will have to take a close look at how you've arranged things.

WHAT YOUR CUSTOMERS EXPECT

One of the main reasons why every marketing, sales, or service manager should be interested in the idea of relationship marketing is that customers are increasingly expecting their relationships with larger companies – and indeed public sector organisations – to be *managed*. They know that they have given a lot of information to these suppliers, whether through their purchases, their payments, when they ask for and receive service, or simply by completing questionnaires. Some customers

Customers expect you to manage your relationship with them.

Table 1.1 *Customer expectations*

Customers Expect	Do you deliver?
When customers require service, they expect details of their relationship with you to be available to whoever is delivering the service, and to be used if relevant	
If they are ordering a product or service, they expect information they have given to you about their needs, not just recently but over the years, to be used to identify which product or service is best for them	
If they are in contact with several different members of your company's staff, they expect the actions of these staff to be coordinated	
They expect you to consider their needs for a relationship, not just for individual transactions within the relationship	
If there are problems on the customers' side, eg meeting payments, service problems which are the customers' fault, they expect their past relationships with you to be taken into consideration	
Loyal customers expect to have better relationships with you than if they were not loyal. They expect loyalty from you	

expect this information to be used to improve how the company manages them. Examples of where they expect the relationship to be managed are included in Table 1.1.

These are just some of the expectations your customers might have. Obviously, not all your customers have all these expectations all of the time, but some have some of them some of the time! As the key to competitive marketing lies in fulfilling relevant customer expectations better than your competitors do, you need to take these expectations seriously. We know that customers who are satisfied with the relationship will not necessarily buy more, and may even buy less if a competitor comes up with a better product or service. But the better the relationship you have with your customers, the more likely they are to have doubts about going to your competitors. Of course, this means finding out what these expectations are, so it is not surprising to discover that one of the earliest milestones on the road to relationship management is research to identify your customer's relationship needs. We cover this in Chapter 2.

THE ROLE OF INFORMATION

In the above list of customer expectations, information about your customers and about the state of the relationship between them and you features prominently. So at the centre of many companies' approach to relationship marketing is the customer database. This should contain information not only on the customer, but also on the relationship (eg transactions, marketing communications sent to the customer, responses, sales calls, etc). The discipline of database marketing, the management and systems required to support it, and its role in relationship marketing, is covered in Chapter 12.

THE ROLE OF PERSONAL CONTACT

Amidst all the media hype about new technology, it is all too easy to forget that relationship marketing is about people and contacts between them. The people include:

- ❏ Your customer – and if the customer is an organisation, all those in the organisation who have dealings with you. For the individual consumer, the role of family and friends must not be forgotten.
- ❏ You, the supplier – not just your sales or service staff, but anyone who has contact with the customer or who affects the relationship with them.
- ❏ Any intermediaries involved in the relationship, eg dealers.

The relationship-transaction-contact hierarchy

A relationship, however long it lasts, can be broken down into a series of perceived transaction periods. These in turn can be broken down into contact episodes, of which a critical element is the contact 'moment of truth', or 'service encounter'.

For example, customers who buy new cars may pay two or three visits to the dealer before buying. They may have several telephone conversations with the dealer before and after the sale. They may exchange one or two letters during the transaction. They may visit the dealer after the sale to have a minor problem rectified.

Throughout this period, most customers are likely to consider themselves engaged in a transaction with the dealer. If this period of transaction is well managed, customers are likely to return to the dealer for service and for a replacement car when the time comes. They may also buy a more expensive model, or buy insurance, extended warranty, or finance through the dealer.

After the purchase transaction is over, the relationship continues, with further transaction periods occurring around the service intervals and then with the next car purchase.

The service encounter

A perceived transaction period may be composed of a number of service encounters. During each service encounter and over the transaction period as a whole, the customer may go through a range of mental states, such as:

- ❑ Experiencing the need.
- ❑ Panic about how to fulfil the need, or whether it will be fulfilled at all.
- ❑ Sensitivity – about whether the right choice has been made, or whether to accept the way in which the service is being provided.
- ❑ Dependence – a feeling of being as a child to the 'adult' provider of service.
- ❑ Happiness or unhappiness – according to the degree of success of the encounter or transaction.
- ❑ Satisfaction or resentment – after the encounter or transaction is over, according to its result.

Understanding what the customer experiences during the service encounter is vital to improving management of the relationship.

THE ROLE OF STRATEGY

Business strategy and planning hold the key to relationship marketing. Your customers are normally confronted by the outcome of a mixture of policies – product, service, staff, invoicing, and so forth. Therefore, the way that these policies affect your customers should be consistent. Otherwise, there is the risk that one aspect of policy may be badly out of line with others.

Relationship marketing is an approach that should pervade your whole organisation.

Relationship marketing is founded partly on your perceptions of your customers. Relationship marketing comes naturally to the market-led company, which highlights customer needs to all parts of the organisation. Of course, relationship marketing is not just part of marketing, but an approach which should pervade your whole organisation. This will only happen if relationship marketing concepts are the foundation for your business plans, structures, and processes.

CUSTOMER ORIENTATION

The dominant principle of relationship marketing is 'customer orientation'. This does not mean giving the customer everything! It *does* mean striving to identify customer needs and meeting them – profitably. Customer orientation is not just an attitude of mind – it is a complete way of working. To achieve this, you must subscribe to the following principles:

1. Your customers are the greatest asset. Without them, you cannot survive. Building and conserving this asset is the central task of your marketing.
2. To do this, you must understand your customers' needs better than your competitors – particularly their relationship needs. You must use this understanding to meet these needs better than your competitors do.
3. You will only be able to understand and meet your customers' relationship needs if you put your customers first. This means managing your day-to-day work to deliver the best results to your customers. Customers do not belong to you by right, but by your staff's hard, customer-oriented work.

Lack of customer orientation is common. Many suppliers are inward-looking, more concerned with solving their own problems of product design, production or sales, or internal politics, rather than the needs of their customers. To be customer-oriented, you must treat customer needs as the foundation of your policy. You must identify customer needs before designing products and services. You must set administrative procedures according to customers' requirements, rather than administrative convenience. You must listen to customers before promoting products and services to them. You must promote in terms of benefits to customers, not features. You must measure success using customer-based measures, such as customer satisfaction indices, responses to marketing campaigns and customer loyalty, as well as sales.

As you become more customer-relationship oriented, you will start to use a variety of measures of success in meeting customer needs. These measures are transformed into targets for managers responsible for different groups of customers. These measures are needed because good customer relationships cannot be achieved without increasing *account-ability* for the state of these relationships.

AVOIDING FAILURE IN RELATIONSHIP MARKETING

Relationship marketing is a dangerous phrase. The idea of relationship marketing seems logical and obvious. Explaining the idea does not take a long time.

The weakness is that most people do not realise that relationship marketing *does* involve reorienting policy, from top to bottom of an organisation. Adding the customer's perspective does complicate things. The main risk to relationship marketing, therefore, is that you will take the idea on board without realising its significance, and then fail to follow it through. Worse, you may hurry it through without working out its full implications. The aim of this book is to encourage you to apply the ideas of relationship marketing slowly and steadily, experiencing benefits all along the way. Without this level-headed approach and long-term commitment, relationship marketing may go badly wrong.

Relationship marketing is a long-term commitment.

In fact, there are very few examples of anything near perfection in relationship marketing. In most cases, it is better to assume that perfection will never be achieved. This is all the more so because many companies' customers change, as they learn from their relationship with the company and other companies. Some customers are leaving, others joining. So relationship marketing is set new challenges all the time. For this reason, it is better to adopt the philosophy of continuous improvement, backed up by periodic measurement of achievement relative to customer needs. This book therefore not only sets out the techniques of relationship management, but suggests a methodology for planning and improving relationship marketing.

THIS BOOK

Customer relationship management is not a panacea for all marketing ills. Nor does it necessarily imply radical change. Just as Molière's Bourgeois Gentilhomme discovered that he was 'speaking prose', so many companies are today discovering that they are 'managing customer relationships' very well. However, there are also many companies which are not. So, unless you can answer 'Yes' to *all* the following questions, you need to consider some of the pointers in this book. You might find Table 1.2, in which our findings about a wide range of companies are also summarised, helpful.

If you can honestly say yes to all of the points in Table 1.2, then this book should just become an *aide-mémoire* to you. As the checklist implies, customer relationship marketing is about matching the type of relationship with customer needs and worth. It is not just about planning, or systems, or people, or setting up a process; or about developing policies to state how customers should be handled. It is all of these things, as this chapter has illustrated and the rest of this book will describe. We have organised the chapters (Table 1.3) into three areas although there is an element of planning, implementation and control in each of them. The current chapter and the next two focus on the relationship-marketing orientation. Chapters 4 to 8 focus on strategic aspects, and the rest of the book on what you need to do at the practical level to improve your relationship marketing.

Table 1.2 *Where do you stand in relationship marketing?*

Are you confident about the following?	Other Companies	You?
Have you identified those groups of customers which contribute most to your profits?	*Common*	
Have you defined what all types of customers want out a relationship with you – what will make them loyal?	*Only done for largest customers usually*	
Have you set customer relationship objectives for your company?	*Rarely*	
Do you know how loyal your key groups of customers are, from all attitudinal and behavioural points of view?	*Rare*	
Do you routinely measure their loyalty and the impact of your marketing, sales and service actions on that loyalty?	*Some measurements common but sporadic use only*	
Are all elements of your marketing, sales and service mix focused on delivering, maintaining and developing relationships with customers? In other words turning the best laid plans into practice?	*Very rarely*	
Do your loyal customers feel that their loyalty is rewarded by you?	*Fairly common in business, less in consumer marketing*	
Do all your staff, and particularly those involved in dealing with customers, understand the concept of customer loyalty and their own role in maintaining and developing it? Is this understanding reinforced by training and motivation?	*Rare*	

Table 1.3 *The book*

	Chapter	
1.	Introduction	*ABOUT CUSTOMER*
2.	Customer relationship marketing from the customer perspective	*RELATIONSHIP*
3.	Customer relationship marketing from your perspective	*MARKETING*
4.	Quantifying the impact	
5.	Customer retention and loyalty	
6.	Planning for customer relationship marketing	*PLANNING THE*
7.	The relationship marketing research process	*APPROACH*
8.	An integrated approach	
9.	Media and campaign planning	
10.	Processes and procedures	
11.	People and performance measurement	*IMPLEMENTATION*
12.	Customer database system implications	*AND CAPABILITY*
13.	Developing the capability	*DEVELOPMENT*

Chapter 2
The Customers' Perspective

Two key questions face you when you are considering whether to adopt the idea of relationship marketing:

1. What types of relationship marketing policy are required?
2. How far should each policy go?

The answers to both these questions lie to a great extent in your customers' needs and perceptions.

CUSTOMER REQUIREMENTS

Customers are reasonable. Many are quite realistic about the relationship you can provide, and know that you are constrained by resources, technology, and the problems of managing change. Customers whose expectations are unrealistic can be educated as to what is realistic.

In analysing your customers' views about their relationship with you, you must understand that the period during which your customers consider themselves to be in a relationship with you may be quite long. Opportunities to strengthen this relationship occur throughout this period, particularly just before, during, and just after your transactions with them.

In their relationship with you, your customers may distinguish between major contact episodes and less important ones. For example, a car being booked in for its annual service may start with a minor contact episode – calling to book the service. The next step may be more significant – telling the service manager what problems the car has got, or putting it in writing. Then comes the day of the service, when the customer leaves the car at the garage. The customer may be worried all day. Uncertainty may be felt about whether the car will be ready in time, whether all faults will be rectified, and what the cost will be. Then comes what is arguably the most important contact of all – when the customer collects the car and pays the bill. Close relationship management at this point is critical. If the car is going to take longer to service, the customer should be telephoned if possible. This will prevent the awful situation of the customer having to wait for the car, which adds to the customer's uncertainty. For example, the customer may wonder whether being told that the car is being waited for will cause service staff to hurry and not do the job properly.

So, your customers' relationship requirements will usually vary according to what *they* consider to be the significance of each transaction with you, and of the overall relationship. In our example of a car service, before booking in the car, the customer may want a list of service items, costs and incentives, and a calendar of available dates. When booking in the car, the customer may require brisk and efficient service. When confronted with the bill, the customer may require careful explanation of why the service cost so much!

LEVELS OF RELATIONSHIP

The idea of the level of relationship your customers expect must be expressed more concisely if you are to base policy on it. We define level of relationship to include:

> ❑ The media through which the contacts take place, eg mail, telephone, face-to-face.
> ❑ The frequency of contacts (and timing may be an important element here).
> ❑ Whom each contact is with (which part of your organisation, which individual, etc).
> ❑ The scope of each contact – what subjects are covered.
> ❑ The information exchanged in each contact.
> ❑ The outcomes of each contact, ie next steps for both the customer and yourself.
> ❑ The cost of each contact to the customer – not just money, but time and stress.

In most cases, customers have an idea about the *minimum acceptable* relationship, and the *desired* level. If customers already have experience of dealing with you, there may also be a *perceived* level – the level they perceive they receive. Perceived levels contrast with *actual* levels, which is a statement from your point of view as to what relationship actions were definitely carried out.

Note that perceptions about contacts (type, frequency, etc) often vary significantly from actual attributes, and are often subject to a *halo effect*. The better a customer's relationship with you, the more positive their perception of each contact. For example, loyal customers may believe that they are in contact more frequently with you than they actually are (perhaps because you are 'front of mind' for them), and may have a more positive view of each contact.

But you may also be providing too much! The best example of this is the *over-attentive* relationship – contact which is too frequent, giving or asking for too much information, etc. In telemarketing, if a customer calls the response-handling centre and the call is answered immediately after the first ring, customers have no time to collect their thoughts after dialling. This 'thought collection' time is particularly important in countries that are switching from older methods of call connection to electronic methods, where the ring follows the dialling much more quickly. If, coupled with this, the telephone operator is too quick and aggressive (from the customers' perspective) with the opening dialogue, customers may feel threatened, and a barrier to future calls will be formed. Older customers may find this particularly difficult to cope with.

Some customers may have *threshold* levels of satisfaction and dissatisfaction. Relationship standards which fall below the threshold may be strongly criticised, but once within the threshold, performance may be taken for granted. There may also be a band of relationship attributes within which they are more or less indifferent.

WHAT DETERMINES THE RELATIONSHIP YOUR CUSTOMERS WANT?

Here are some of the factors that determine the kind of relationship customers want.

The effect of experience

Customers form requirements and perceptions as a result of several influences. The most important of these is experience, whether with you, a competitor, or some other 'benchmark' company. All suppliers of products and services are in some sense in competition with each other when it comes to relationship marketing. In a consumerist age, it is not unusual to hear customers making explicit comparisons, say, between a retail store and British Rail.

The extent to which customers make such 'parallel comparisons' has been increased by the consumerist values of our age. As leading commercial organisations improve their relationship marketing, so public service organisations are under pressure to do the same. This is because customers *do* compare and form expectations which are transferred across different suppliers of products and services.

In a competitive environment, customers who stay in relationships with particular suppliers do so because the total package they receive from the supplier – product, service, price, credit, relationship marketing and so forth – is right for them. But there is no room for complacency. Customers of low price suppliers may have 'talked themselves into' accepting the idea that low relationship standards are worth tolerating because of the low price charged. However, if competition emerges based on low prices but high standards of relationship marketing, customer requirements may change.

Behaviour may lag behind experience. A supplier with a good relationship record may occasionally lapse. Perhaps surprisingly, its customers do not immediately switch suppliers. They have learnt that their supplier has provided good experiences in the past. This learning takes time to undo. This customer behaviour gives suppliers the opportunity to recover.

Word of mouth

The power of word of mouth is often quoted in terms of how satisfied or dissatisfied customers communicate their experience to others. Customers who are totally satisfied, or who are dissatisfied and then have their problems resolved by you, can become powerful *advocates* for you. They will recommend you to their friends. If the latter are dissatisfied with *their* supplier, then the recommendations can be particularly effective.

Customers can become powerful advocates for you.

The force of recommendation is as powerful in organisational markets as in customer markets. Information about relationships may be communicated within the buying centre – the group of staff who make or influence the buying decision – and to other buying centres. In buying centres that are making important, high-risk decisions, it is particularly important for members of the buying centre to be *and to appear* knowledgeable. Any piece of information about the experience of others is often seized upon and given great status.

The time problem

Despite shorter working hours and longer holidays, many customers are *less* tolerant of the time it takes to interact with a supplier. Perceived scarcity of free time can make customers want to achieve more in a short time. This can also make your customers worry about the differences between what they want to achieve and what they actually achieve, and of course what others achieve.

If your customers feel they are short of time, saving their time may be an important relationship proposition. However, the time problem varies by age group. The older and richer the customer, the less the perception of the time problem. Marketers focusing on older customers may well promote the length of time they are prepared to spend with the customer. This applies particularly for more up-market products.

The buying decision

The nature of the buying decision can be classified using the 'Buygrid', a concept borrowed from industrial marketing. It defines certain 'buy-classes', as follows:

- ❑ *New task.* The customer has no experience of the product or service type. In this case, the customer will need a lot of information, and may ask friends or colleagues about it. You are trying to make the sale and establish a relationship at the same time – not an easy task. If you push too hard to make the sale, your later relationship with customers may be poor, because they may have been sold the wrong product or service.
- ❑ *Straight rebuy.* A routine re-order without any modification, often handled routinely. If you are already supplying to a particular customer, your key relationship marketing objective is to facilitate re-ordering, but also to ensure that your customer considers what else they can buy from you at the same time.
- ❑ *Modified rebuy.* The customer seeks to change supplier or some other aspect of the purchase, but wants the same general kind of product or service. Modified rebuys often provide the greatest test of the quality of relationship marketing. Your customer is considering whether to switch products or services, and may switch away from you if you mismanage the relationship with them.

High involvement and low involvement decisions

Many purchases require little or no explanation. Often, purchase motivation is already understood. In others there is little that *needs* to be understood. This is particularly true of routine purchases, eg a bus trip by a customer who makes the same trip every day. Basic products and services are *commodities*. They are purchased for functional reasons and carry little or no symbolic meaning. Their unit price is low, whichever brand is selected. They are routinely purchased. The risk a customer takes by making the wrong choice of supplier or product is low because economic, psychological and social commitment to the product is low. These are *low involvement* products. However, not all low-price, frequently purchased products or services are low involvement products. Commuting journeys by train are certainly not!

Customers sometimes feel that there is a high psychological and social risk of making the wrong choice. This applies particularly when the choice is 'worn' or the experience shared with others. Many products are 'worn' – not just clothes, but also cigarettes, alcohol, cars, books, home furnishings, and the like. These are *high involvement* products and services. These are particularly important for relationship marketing. Good relationship marketing in high involvement situations greatly reinforces customer loyalty. Poor relationship marketing in such situations leads to customer disloyalty and strong word of mouth condemnation.

If a decision is important to the customer, then considerable thought may be devoted to the purchase. If the product is bought frequently, more thinking is likely to take place when the customer is considering switching between suppliers or products. Once the new purchasing pattern is established as a habit, purchases are likely to take place routinely, without much thought.

Stage of the buying cycle

Usually, customers go through the stages illustrated in Figure 2.1 – sometimes sequentially, sometimes with different stages combined:

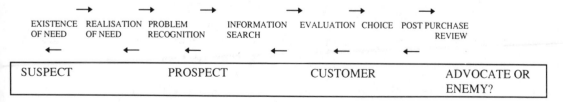

Figure 2.1   The buying cycle

❏ *Existence of the need.* The need comes into existence. Your customer may not be aware of it, but it is there.

❏ *Identification or realisation of need.* The need comes to the 'front of mind'.

❏ *Problem recognition.* The need exists for a reason, typically a problem that needs to be solved (eg meeting a want). Your customer recognises that the problem exists.

❏ *Search for information.* Your customer seeks information about products and services to solve the problem. This is triggered by the need for problem resolution.

❏ *Evaluation.* All the relevant accessible information required to make the choice which will resolve the problem is gathered and analysed. Your customer may or may not have established choice criteria. Even if the criteria are already established, during evaluation they may change. Patterns of deliberation are also important. Some customers rely more on personal advice than on information provided by suppliers. So the outcome of the evaluation depends on various factors, varying from personality and past experience to the way different suppliers provide information.

You must understand the criteria your customers use to evaluate different suppliers, products, and services. This is the link between relationship marketing and financial success. For if the relationship determines choice between suppliers, products, and services, then the commercial justification for investing in creating and managing the relationship is not difficult to produce.

❏ *Choice.* Some choices are impulsive, or at least seem so to others. But many are deliberate and rational, based upon systematic processing of information. Such processing leads first to the formation of an intention to purchase, which is determined by the formulation of beliefs about the product and its likely performance.

❏ *Post-purchase review.* After the decision, your customer re-evaluates it in the light of any new information, eg information about product performance. In some post-purchase situations, customers experience cognitive dissonance, ie they feel unhappy about what they now know. They may experience doubt, even anxiety, if the product did not come up to expectations. This may be resolved in various ways. They may look for information which supports their decision, eg others who made the same decision. They may focus on the 'good deal' they got in an attempt to convince themselves that they made the right decision. They may even ignore, avoid, or distort incoming information which is inconsistent with what they want to believe.

Relationship marketing after the sale can help your customers justify the decision they made, even if there are problems after the sale.

Branding and customer loyalty

When it comes to the purchase, corporate and product/service branding are very important. But they also have a strong effect on your customers' expectations and perceptions of their relationship with you. A strong brand, developed over a long period, gives the relationship a strong platform. Without it, the relationship almost has to start from scratch with every transaction.

Customer loyalty and branding are closely connected. Highly visible and positive branding cannot exist without customer loyalty, and customer loyalty depends on the relationship, in the long run. If you manage relationships with your customers well, they will tend to be loyal, and this will provide the opportunity for branding to get to work. Branding requires the strong imprinting of ideas about the product in customers' minds. These ideas will be positive if customers frequently have good experiences in buying and using your products or services, and good communications with you.

The key manifestation of disloyalty is when a customer switches suppliers or brands. Sometimes this occurs when your customers decide they need a change, not because of any problem with what they are buying from you or how you manage the relationship with them; they are simply in search of variety or a different specification. This cannot be avoided, although good relationship marketing can encourage such customers to return. Switches due to big price differences are also hard to prevent through relationship marketing, unless the cheaper product is lower quality.

Switches due to problems with your product or service, or poor relationship marketing by you, can and should be avoided. The unresolved problem that you do not know about is the most dangerous. It festers, and eventually your customer switches away. Relationship marketing that encourages complaints and ensures that complaints are dealt with well is the best defence against this cause of switching.

The problem that you do not know about is the most dangerous.

Control

Your customers will often be motivated by a need for security. This may lead to a need to be in control of their relationship with you. However, many relationship situations create a perception among customers that they are totally without control, eg the unsolicited telesales call in the evening, which the customer does not know how to terminate.

So, every attempt should be made to explore how to give customers who wish to be in control the feeling of control. The idea of *locus of control* is useful for analysing this situation. In many marketing situations, the locus of control is with you. You determine which marketing actions will take place, and when. But as with all marketing, it is the perceived locus of control that is more important than the actual locus of control. Customers can be persuaded to think that they are in control.

If your customers' control is less than they want – or indeed if they feel they are being asked to control a situation when they are incapable of doing so (eg unqualified, without the right information), levels of stress can rise. This can result in anxious and uncooperative behaviour. Research shows that the need for control does not depend on obvious factors, such as the customer's purchasing power. It is a complex mixture of elements that has as much to do with the customer's individual personality as any other factor. So you need to give the customer the degree of control they want, ie give real control, or take over control yourself. If a new product requires, for its success, for customers to be in control (eg because of a high self-service element), then customer education must be a key part of the product launch package. The nature of the education package will, of course, vary with the ability of target customers to absorb such instructions.

Some customers prefer to be in complete control. However, the same customer who prefers self-service for a routine sales transaction may prefer your close attention for a more complicated transaction. Some customers do not want to be in control. Their need for security may be best fulfilled by cocooning them, so that they do not have to take any initiative. Wherever possible, you should offer the two main options – control or be managed.

Automation

Relationship marketing can be delivered through a variety of media, depending on the nature of the contact. Information can be provided face-to–face, on the telephone, via the Internet or other electronic media, on a video screen, on a TV through video on demand, through a loudspeaker, or in print.

Replacement of people-based by automated relationship marketing provides a challenge to relationship delivery. The best examples of this are in simple transactions. These include:

❑ Telephone directory enquiries or provision of other information through an automated helpline.
❑ Self-service petrol and car-wash.
❑ Video hire through a machine.

These transactions are handled best if you examine the full range of customer needs that need to be satisfied by the automated approach. Often, while carrying out a simple transaction, customers take the opportunity to check facts or receive information. When withdrawing or crediting money, a customer may seek information about account balances or about the clearing of recent transactions. Video cassette renters might seek information about the popularity of certain videos. Sometimes, such information can be provided automatically as part of the transaction.

Following the script

In many relationship situations, your staff are trained to follow a script. Customers can also be trained or educated to expect a script and then to follow it. If customers agree to follow the script, their chance of the transaction and relationship being successful increases, because the script is designed to identify their needs and then guide them through receiving the right response from you. This is at its most explicit in a telemarketing script. If your customers can be conditioned to expect questions to identify their needs, and then to cooperate in subsequent actions to ensure that the contact succeeds, then both you and your customers' objectives will be reached.

Customers who prefer to be in control must be handled more carefully, and systems and scripts designed and staff trained so that these customers believe they are scripting the situation, even though you are in control of the logic and the coverage of the script.

For customers who want control, this may be the single most important part of the relationship 'mix'.

Customers still have a tendency to ignore the script. Perhaps the best example of this is failure to read instructions – the part of the script that precedes human intervention. This may be because this early part of the script is badly written or presented. It is more likely to be that once customers need to be in contact, they prefer human media to printed media.

Some companies use expert computer systems to help manage the dialogue with different kinds of customer and in different service situations. Obviously, this is easiest in telephone-contact situations, but the approach is also used to provide instant simulations of the outcomes of different financial arrangements (eg life insurance, pension) or the costs and benefits of different major computer configurations.

ORGANISING CUSTOMER ANALYSIS

This chapter has shown the variety of attitudes that your customers may have in relation to relationship marketing, and how these attitudes are affected by the nature of the buying process. In Chapter 3, our focus switches to you – the supplier.

Chapter 3

Your Perspective

THE NEED FOR A SECOND LOOK

Until this point, relationship marketing issues have been viewed through your customers' eyes. This chapter sees them through your eyes.

Most managers would agree that in the long run, a close relationship with customers is important to success. But in the short run, your organisational structures, control processes, procedures and operational necessities often bring you and your customers into conflict. The secret of competitive relationship marketing does not, therefore, lie in programmes that only deal with the immediate interface between your customers and you. Relationship marketing, which works in both short and long runs, usually requires you to reconsider every aspect of policy.

PLANNING FOR RELATIONSHIP MARKETING

Your ability to meet customers' relationship needs depends upon several factors as illustrated in Figure 3.1 and described below:

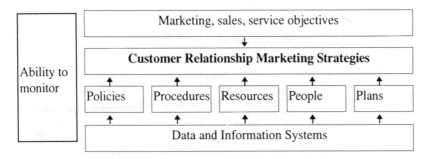

Figure 3.1   Planning for relationship marketing

❑ *Your objectives.* What you aim to achieve and whether these objectives require customer relationships to be managed.
❑ *Your strategies.* The translation of objectives into the main lines of policy.
❑ *Your policies and action plans.* The translation of strategies into practical work.
❑ *Your process and procedures.* The norms and rules by which your staff work.
❑ *Your resources.* Allocated to assist the achievement of different policies.
❑ *Your people.* They contribute so much to relationship marketing. If they are wrongly assigned, managed, or trained, their effect on customer relationship can be devastating.
❑ *Your planning processes.* They match your resources to objectives and harness resources through particular policies, working to particular procedures.
❑ *Your systems.* The right data available to the right people at the right time will enable your management process to happen.
❑ Your ability to *monitor* key performance indicators.

These are introduced here and discussed in the next few chapters. The effect of each of the above on relationship marketing depends on whether your focus on customer needs is maintained. This in turn depends on how you use customer information.

THE ROLE OF CUSTOMER INFORMATION

Information about your customers and their needs should be taken into account during the planning process and should be available in a useable form at specified points of contact with the customer. These points of contact may be inbound (the customer contacts you) or outbound (you contact the customer) across a variety of contact types (eg orders, complaints, general enquiries, sales enquiries, billing queries, technical queries). Using data in this way, for both planning and communication purposes, is important in 'delivering the strategy' and making your plans more visible to your customers.

SYSTEMS, PROCEDURES, SCRIPTS, AND BOUNDARIES

The idea of the 'script' governing the relationship between you and your customers is an essential part of relationship marketing (see page 37). What you see as a set of procedures should be thought of as a customer script (not necessarily something to control the flow of one conversation, but something to control the overall dialogue), for situations in which the customer is interacting with you. If the script is followed, there is a reasonable assurance that the quality of the outcome of the transaction or relationship will be as required. The script therefore needs to be worked out carefully, communicated to your customers and, where necessary, form the basis of customer training (for complex scripts).

The script is also a way of giving your customers a perceived level of control. For if your customers learn the script properly, the contact episode can be effectively managed by them. A good script can make your customer feel that the outcome of the episode is more predictable too, reducing stress levels (for example, if the script begins with them providing their customer number, all data can be on-hand). Of course, not all your customers require a high degree of control, so a script may not be necessary if each service episode is managed with close personal service.

LEARNING FROM EXPERIENCE

Knowledge is the key to relationship marketing. This knowledge is of two kinds:

Knowledge is the key to relationship marketing.

---

1. Knowledge of your customers – what they currently perceive, need and expect and how this situation may change in the future.
2. Knowledge of your own organisation – its capabilities, what it actually delivers to your customers, and how both of these will be affected by future policies.

Knowledge of customers

Knowledge of customers comes in many ways. These include:

❑ Formal market research and observation.
❑ Transaction information – responses and enquiries, sales, etc.
❑ Competitive information – what your customers are buying from other suppliers.
❑ Complaints and compliments.
❑ Feedback from your customer-facing staff.

The key issue here is whether your organisation is sufficiently customer-oriented, ie does it demand and thrive upon feedback from customers? Or does it regard customer information as an intrusion to its work? Relationship marketing cannot thrive without a thirst for customer feedback and without a proper process for taking this feedback, digesting it and identifying from it any opportunities for improving relationship marketing.

Knowledge of your own organisation

The two key questions that need to be answered here are:

1. How is your organisation *structured* to deliver relationship marketing?

2. How is your organisation *managed* to deliver relationship marketing?

In a large organisation, with many tiers of management, or with many branches or subsidiaries, these questions must be asked at each level.

Structuring to deliver relationship marketing is a question of putting authority to deal with individual customers as close to your customers as possible, while concentrating responsibility for relationship management in that part of your organisation that has both the resources to invest in achieving it and the information flows to monitor and measure its achievement.

'Closeness' does not necessarily imply geographical proximity. Many national suppliers have found that for handling individual relationships, central telemarketing facilities are more cost-effective than having many offices around the country dealing with customers part-time.

Many suppliers – large and small – have also found that a key element of relationship marketing is to make it easy for customers to contact them. Until customers find this easy, it is almost impossible to judge what relationship is being delivered. This is because customers may be largely cut-off from the organisation, except when the latter wants to contact them.

Managing to deliver relationship marketing is a question of having systems, management procedures and control processes that allow staff to meet customer needs, and recruiting, training and keeping staff informed so that they have the skills and capability to meet your customer needs – the focus of the last part of this book.

Warning signs of relationship management failures include those in Table 3.1. Tick one or more of these and it will identify an area to work on.

LEARNING IN PRACTICE: THE ROLE OF LEADERSHIP

It is one thing to have lots of data and ideas about how to manage customer relationships. It is another to do something about it. This is where relationship marketing leadership comes in. Ideally, in every organisation that depends on dealing successfully with customers, all staff should be relationship marketing-oriented. However, getting to such a situation is not easy. Change normally requires leadership. In a large organisation, this leadership is required at every level. Leaders function as coach, communicator, and monitor. They identify problems, propose solutions, and motivate people to change. They initiate

Table 3.1   *Relationship warning signs*

Are any of these warning signs apparent in your situation?

Needing to refer too many individual relationship management decisions to senior managers

Long lead times for YES/NO decisions on customer requests

Systems not allowing staff the flexibility to deal with customer needs, causing miscommunication or delays

Work pressures not allowing staff to complete tasks (customers often go to the end of the queue in such circumstances) or forcing staff to focus on formal processes, not customers

Poor quality information being given to staff, so that they do not know what to tell your customers

Motivation, appraisal and other people-management systems giving inadequate attention and reward to success in dealing with customers

Complaint rates rising

Front-line staff motivation low and/or turnover high

Customer loss rates increasing!

programmes to implement changes to systems and procedures. Without a good sprinkling of relationship marketing champions around the organisation, even the best relationship marketing policies are likely to fail.

THE RELATIONSHIP MARKETING LEADER

The first role of the relationship marketing leader is to make sure that the learning is properly absorbed by the organisation. This means taking the conclusions to the right people and showing the evidence that relationship marketing pays (or satisfies some other basic objective). This may mean demonstrating the severity of the problem, or the competitive opportunity.

At this stage things can go badly wrong. For once an organisation, however large or small, has accepted the need for improvements to relationship marketing, the next step is definitely *not* a relationship marketing programme. The next step is to take the idea and benefits of relationship marketing into the core policy-making process, and ensure it does its work there. Once the idea and methods of relationship marketing are absorbed into this process, then relationship marketing leadership works within the procedures and systems of every department, not as a challenge to them.

THE IMPORTANCE OF A CLEAR CORPORATE STRATEGY

It is easy for an organisation to become confused about relationship marketing. The 'headless chicken' analogy – running around in every direction without a clear goal – is a perfect fit. Today, relationship marketing consultants are two a penny. Articles extolling the virtues of relationship marketing are part of the daily diet of managers. In this situation, a manager might rush into an ill-considered relationship marketing programme. This would be exactly the wrong thing to do.

Relationship marketing is one approach to looking at how your organisation works. Whether the relationship marketing perspective is the correct one depends upon what your objectives are, how you aim to achieve them, and with which customers. You can only determine whether you should be investing more time and money in relationship marketing through a proper analysis, which is part of your normal planning process. However, a clear corporate strategy involving anything other than lip service to customer relationship marketing is unlikely without influential members of senior management being committed to the concept.

GAINING COMMITMENT TO RELATIONSHIP MARKETING

Before we move on to describe the essential elements of *planning* relationship marketing, it should be said that there are several requirements you must fulfil to be able to deliver relationship marketing. There is little chance of sustaining delivery of relationship marketing if only one or a few of these requirements are fulfilled. For this reason, it is very important for your whole organisation – however large or small – to be committed to managing relationships with customers.

In a small organisation – even a one-man business – there is less chance for great variations in attitude between members of staff. If the owner or manager is not committed to managing relationships with customers, this attitude will transfer quickly to other staff. There will be a close connection between staff behaviour and success according to the owner's or manager's criteria.

In a large supplier, staff working with customers cannot maintain standards of relationship marketing which are not underwritten by the formal policies of their organisation. The more remote these staff are from the centre of power, and the more freedom they are allowed, the longer such behaviour can continue. Eventually, however, resource pressures are likely to constrain this behaviour. However, in a large organisation, staff in contact with customers may be totally unconcerned about them.

In such situations, the lead from top management is crucial. Without it, all down the line, managers will be faced with other priorities. These include things such as short-term cost control or immediate sales achievement, avoidance of risk by sticking to procedures, and the like. Staff working close to customers need strong and frequent reinforcement if they are to stick to the principles of relationship marketing.

Staff working close to customers need strong and frequent reinforcement.

Strategic focus is essential to the success of relationship marketing. But strategic focus by itself is not enough. Your top management must also be committed to the role of relationship marketing in achieving the desired focus and in contributing to competitive positioning. If relationship marketing is considered as insignificant relative to return on assets, and as making only a marginal contribution to it, then there is little hope for its survival. The message will be clearly transmitted down the line!

Too much has been written and spoken about 'top management commitment' for any line manager to suspend their suspicion when they hear or see the phrase. It is a hack phrase – and therefore a warning sign. Commitment means commitment to resources and to seeing policies through, particularly in adversity. It is easy to subscribe to slogans. It is more difficult to implement policies that require fundamental changes of attitude. It takes time as well as money. Therefore, when the term 'top management commitment' is used here, it refers to considered commitment by top management. For this commitment to be true, top managers must have full knowledge of the time and resources that will be absorbed, and the problems that will be encountered along the way – particularly those relating to staff attitudes and skills.

This implies that genuine commitment must be preceded by clear communication of the costs (financial and other) as well as the benefits of relationship marketing. Where the situation allows, it should also be based on hard evidence as to the benefits, eg pilot studies.

Basing commitment on understanding

It is not sensible to ask your top management to be committed to relationship marketing unless they understand:

❑ your organisation's current relationship with your customers;
❑ how it can be improved;
❑ the costs and benefits of improving it.

It therefore makes sense to involve your senior management in some of the activities that usually form the 'front end' of a commitment to relationship marketing. It is not realistic to expect commitment other than on the basis of understanding. You should involve your senior management in research into customer and staff attitudes. This should not be just through presentation of results. Table 3.2 illustrates ways to involve top management.

Table 3.2   *Involving top management*

Which activities will appeal to your senior management?

Attendance at focus groups or meetings of user groups

Visits (to own and competitive sites)

Exposing them to the relationship provided by your company and your competitors

Involvement in research design and interpretation

Exposure to examples of successful and unsuccessful relationship marketing programmes. The latter are important, as they indicate that such programmes are not easy to develop and run. Exposure should include performance indicators and financial results

Continuity of commitment

The idea that commitment must be sustained has already been mentioned. Sustaining commitment to ideas that seem very attractive is a problem. New ideas come along and replace them. You should always treat claims for the universal applicability of a concept with suspicion, demand hard evidence and insist on piloting. This is a solid foundation – and the only foundation – for relationship marketing. Once such a foundation is built, it provides the basis for an enduring commitment.

Depth of commitment

Finally, the commitment must be deep, in the sense that it leads to the concept of relationship marketing permeating all plans and delivery of those plans. This, of course, requires transfer of the commitment to those building the plans and implementing them.

This raises few problems when the drive for top management commitment has come from 'the troops' – in this case middle managers. But it does raise problems when the commitment results from a top manager's own conviction, a private 'journey to Damascus', perhaps stimulated by consultants. In such cases, a programme of communication and education may be required. In particular, the 'seasoned operators' who form the core of the delivery apparatus may feel, with some justification, they have 'seen it all before'. These operators – sales people, counter staff, etc – will have been subjected to many campaigns over the years. The situation will be worse if these campaigns were short lived, with no real benefit to the operators, disappearing like a Will O' The Wisp as soon as the environment changed.

To avoid this, relationship marketing programmes must provide benefits – immediate and longer term. This must be not only for staff responsible for implementing them with customers, but also for all staff in the line of command. The steady transmission of the philosophy and practices of relationship marketing down the line is a much better solution that a quick blast of publicity with no follow-through. This implies that you must pace your approach to relationship marketing. The approach must be durable, with steady annual improvements in the relationship and in resulting profitability.

Commitment without strain!

It is not realistic to expect senior managers to live, eat and breathe relationship marketing all the time. They have many other responsibilities. Their role in developing and supporting relationship marketing must therefore be closely defined. The role of senior management is indicated in Table 3.3.

Table 3.3   *Senior management commitment*

As a senior manager, do you . . . ?

Provide overall direction and guidance

Set relationship marketing objectives and define quality standards

Support these standards by meeting regularly with staff to discuss problems and opportunities in relation to the standards

Create a style of teamwork that encourages staff to take responsibility for relationship marketing and work together to improve it

Act as a role model (particularly through visiting company locations)

Accept responsibility for the quality of relationship marketing

Help evaluate staff ideas on how to improve relationship marketing

Help create a culture of orderly routine, within which your relationship marketing objectives can more easily be met

Ensure that time is spent with new employees to introduce them to your culture and support them in their attempts to build and sustain customer relationships

More than this should not be required. But for some companies, this role would be a radical departure from the norm. In service industries, the culture of relationship marketing is often readily accepted. But in industries that survive by selling physical products, particularly where contact with customers is infrequent, much of the focus of senior management is on current sales levels and the performance of sales staff.

Relationship marketing often takes a back seat, to the customer's misfortune. If senior management in these industries are to take on the kind of responsibilities listed above, it is all the more important for them to go through the kind of exposure to relationship marketing outlined above.

PERFORMANCE INDICATORS

If commitment to relationship marketing is not translated into the way staff are measured or managed, then little will change. If your managers and staff hear messages about commitment, but see no change in the way that their performance is judged, they will be deeply suspicious of the message. Some early move to change performance indicators in the direction indicated by the relationship marketing concept is therefore recommended.

The acid test of these indicators, from top management's point of view, is how top management reacts when relationship marketing performance indicators clash with others, eg financial. Of course, if your company is profit-oriented, and profits suddenly go deeply into the red, there is every excuse for focusing on indicators which relate to short-term profitability. Without survival, you will not have relationships with any customers tomorrow. Despite this, however, there are different ways of reacting to a crisis.

Integrating performance indicators

Your top management has a particularly important role when it comes to integrating financial, technical, and relationship marketing indicators. One of the problems that many suppliers face is split responsibilities for achieving the following tasks:

❏ Delivering quality according to specifications (ie technical performance).
❏ Delivering financial performance (eg profits or satisfying a budget constraint).
❏ Achieving relationships with customers that satisfy the latter.

For example, in a large industrial equipment company:

❏ Financial staff may be responsible for pricing, setting credit terms and chasing debtors (whether for equipment sales or after-sales service).
❏ Engineers may be responsible for performance of installed equipment.

❏ Marketing and sales staff may be responsible for finding new customers and getting more business out of existing customers.

Each group potentially has a strong influence on relationship marketing, but can end up pulling in opposite directions. Financial staff may alienate customers by chasing debtors. Service engineers may create dissatisfaction by questioning customers' choice of equipment ('who sold you this, then?'). Sales staff may respond to inventory shortages by selling equipment not suitable for the customers' use, raising service costs and creating customer dissatisfaction.

The lines of control through which these different staff are managed may only merge near the top of the organisation. Top management must insist that the performance of these staff is assessed partly on the basis of their help in achieving overall customer satisfaction, through their own actions, or their impacts on the actions of their colleagues in other departments. For example, attitude surveys should be used to provide information enabling the organisation to correlate treatment of debtors with later sales levels.

Resource allocation

A final test of top management commitment is whether it is translated into resource. Throughout this book, the view is that in the end, relationship marketing pays for itself. However, in the short term, an investment may be required before a return is achieved. This investment may be in the form of training, systems, or even refunds to customers. Of course, it is only fair to top management not to demand allocation of resources without evidence of benefits. But once evidence has been accepted, then the commitment should stay.

Quantifying the impact is the next key task.

Chapter 4
Quantifying the Impact

ACCOUNTABILITY IN MARKETING

The adoption of relationship marketing has many long-term effects on your business. For example, measurability of results can make your marketing function fully accountable for all its expenditure. Business results can be traced back to activities and benefits set against costs. Measurability also makes it easier to test the effectiveness of different approaches, giving the marketing function the tools to improve results.

However, accountability creates pressures within marketing. In many companies, the marketing function is not truly accountable for all its policies. It may be accountable in a general sense, but the information may simply not be available to hold marketing accountable for particular policies. For example, the results of a change in promotional policy or in salesforce compensation may not be accurately measurable. Relationship marketing changes this.

The question 'how much is relationship marketing worth'? is shorthand for three further questions:

1. How much is a 'properly marketed-to' customer worth?
2. How much difference does good relationship marketing make?
3. What is the strategic versus tactical application of relationship marketing techniques?

HOW MUCH IS A 'PROPERLY-MARKETED TO' CUSTOMER WORTH?

'Lifetime value of the customer' is not a new concept. Its pedigree comes from direct marketing (especially mail order), where long-term customer behaviour is the key to success, and calculating the difference between costs of acquiring customers and the benefits and costs of retention is the norm. The concept is also widely used in consumer goods brand management, where the key calculation is how much to spend to prevent consumers from brand switching.

Calculating the value of a customer is logically simple – the key is data. The required process is as follows:

❑ Determine your target customers.
❑ Identify the costs of gaining and maintaining customers, and of selling additional products and services to them.
❑ Identify the profit contribution arising from the sales made.
❑ Subtract one from the other to produce a stream of net contribution over the years.
❑ Use discounted cash flow techniques to find customers' net present value.

Using historical data of customers you already have, lifetime value (LTV) can be calculated and then extrapolated, making adjustments where necessary. Some companies are very uncomfortable about using past data as a predictor of future purchase behaviour. However, in many markets it has proved the most reliable method of forecasting. An example of an LTV calculation can be found below.

1. Choose a segment of customers (c.1000) who fit a defined set of criteria and who were recruited (gained) at the same time. The time period is not critical. If your records only go back two years then so be it. Ideally, pick a five-year period.
2. Extract the revenues that have been generated by those 1000 customers each year (by campaign, season, or period – if you can – but it is usually not critical).
3. Calculate, or estimate, the annual marketing and sales cost of managing those customers. Usually a campaign cost and an apportioned cost of (field) selling will be sufficient to start with if historical records are not accurate on a per customer basis.
4. Calculate the contribution per year.
5. Apply a discounted cash flow percentage (normally available from Finance Departments for the calculation of financial returns on large projects) to calculate the LTV each year for the 1000 customers (net present value).
6. Divide the total by the number of customers to find out a 'per customer' value.
7. Model the figures, assuming you did things differently, to look at the sensitivity of the LTV. This may involve an extra campaign per year, an increase in retention rate of 2 per cent, a reduction in the cost of

selling if an extra product is sold into 25 per cent of the base, etc. This 'what-if' type analysis will indicate where the biggest effect is found. This figure can then be used to determine how much to spend on relationship marketing to each group of customers.

WHAT DOES 'PROPERLY-MARKETED TO' MEAN?

'Properly marketed to' means that you have:

❑ identified the customer's needs;
❑ developed appropriate products and services to meet those needs ('appropriate' meaning consistent with your business strategy and profit objectives);
❑ marketed them to the customer, with appropriate prices, channels of distribution, presentation and marketing communications.

Good marketing and relationship marketing are not the same thing.

Good marketing and customer relationship marketing are not the same thing. For example, if you sell the wrong type of product to customers, or if you try to manage them through the wrong distribution channel, you'll be less likely to satisfy them, however much you invest in relationship marketing. If they have a choice, they are unlikely to come back to you.

Your marketing plan, phrased in terms of its impact upon your customers, should tell you the minimum customer LTV you are trying to create. However, if your marketing has not been properly focused on customers, or if your relationship marketing is weak, your marketing plan will only represent a minimum LTV. So your marketing plan should be revised when you have been through the entire relationship marketing calculation.

HOW MUCH DIFFERENCE DOES GOOD RELATIONSHIP MARKETING MAKE?

The answer to this depends on precisely how you do your relationship marketing and on how your customers react to your relationship marketing initiatives. There are no absolutes here – every company is different, and every group of customers is different. The effect of good relationship marketing can only be identified through research. This research will typically identify:

❑ *What kinds of contact customers* **perceive** *they have with your company.* This is called the contact audit. Its results often surprise managers, because they discover that their customers are in contact or attempted contact with their company far more often and in a greater variety of ways than they believed possible. Further, their customers may often think about contact but be dissuaded by the difficulty of achieving it!

❏ *What the outcomes of these contacts are, in terms of the relationship.* Research is likely to produce a complex picture here. In simple terms, a positive outcome leads to improved relationship marketing, but 'positive outcome' can relate to many policy areas, such as use of the right contact media, the right frequency and quality of contact, use of customer information to provide the right solution, 'right first time' solution of problems, and also well-handled complaints – a negative outcome followed by a positive outcome.

❏ *How customers react to these outcomes.* Once again, the picture is likely to be complex. For example, well-handled complaints or time taken to adjust a product to a customer's needs may reinforce purchasing behaviour more than no-problem contacts or products which are from the beginning absolutely right for the customer. This is usually because when your customers complain, they receive higher quality attention than normal. Worse, it may be because the only time they receive your attention is when they complain! Also, you should be interested not only in customers that are directly affected, but also those who are told by your customers about how well you handle them. Satisfaction leads to recommendation to others, but satisfaction after good problem-resolution may lead to stronger recommendation than routinely good service! The key here is to estimate changes in lifetime buying behaviour – of the customers affected and of those they tell about it. Naturally, estimates are more accurate the longer your company has been measuring the connection between good relationship marketing and buying and recommending behaviour. However, the key need here is not for 100 per cent accuracy, but for a broad understanding of the longer-term profit implications of success-ful relationships.

❏ *What the financial consequences are.* This is the translation of customers' relationship-affected buying behaviour into profit, as per the methodo-logy described above.

TACTICAL VERSUS STRATEGIC APPLICATION OF RELATIONSHIP MARKETING

Some of the techniques of relationship marketing may be used just as tactical weapons. However, you can use relationship marketing more effectively by taking a strategic approach, and transforming how you do business. The strategic factors which must be considered in payback calculations are summarised in Table 4.1 and described in more detail below.

Table 4.1 *Strategic impact of relationship marketing*

Through relationship marketing, do you think you will achieve . . .

Competitive superiority?

Provision of alternative sales channels?

Setting up barriers to competitive market entry?

Ability to develop new products and services and get them to the market more quickly?

If any one of these are ticked, relationship marketing must be viewed as a strategic approach to the business, and not simply justified as a 'campaign by campaign' selling tool.

Competitive superiority

You can establish competitive superiority by building and exploiting a database with comprehensive coverage of your existing and potential customers for your current and future products and services. You might use this capability aggressively, to win customers from your competition (conquest sales), eg by regular mailings to your competitors' customers. Such mailings can ask for information about customer needs. This information can then be used to design products and marketing programmes.

Competitive superiority can also be established through lower costs. In many industries, the field salesperson can only make between two and five calls per day (although in some industries the norm may be ten). A telemarketer can make between 20 and 50 decision-maker contacts per day. The optimum competitive policy is to use field sales and telemarketing according to their relative strengths, using a customer database to coordinate the two.

Thus the salesforce can be used where the face-to-face call is needed. This is likely to be where:

❑ Personal service is considered essential.
❑ An important new contact is being made.
❑ A difficult and sensitive problem needs to be solved.
❑ A complex presentation needs to be made.
❑ In-depth diagnostic work needs to be carried out.
❑ The customer asks for a sales visit.
❑ On-site research is required.

A telemarketing team working off the customer database can be used for all other calls. Eventually, with appropriate teamwork between the field salesforce, the telemarketing team *and the customer* (whose time is also valuable and therefore who wants to be contacted by the most effective means for each call), more complex objectives can be handled by the telemarketing team. The telemarketer may become a full account manager. This approach increases the quantity and quality of contact between the salesforce and customers, without increasing the cost. It also provides greater flexibility, enabling sales effort to be redeployed more quickly to meet competitive challenges. The discipline with which sales effort is managed can be increased. For example, it can be marshalled in a more disciplined manner to mount competitive attacks on customers known to be dissatisfied with a competitive product.

Neglected customers are a problem for most businesses. In many industrial product or service markets, small business customers may be neglected. In consumer markets, neglected customers may be isolated households or households with low purchasing frequencies. For both groups, the costs of traditional sales channels may preclude contact that is frequent enough to reinforce buying behaviour. The customer may eventually switch to competitive products, assuming that your competitors have not fallen into the same trap!

Neglected customers are a problem for most businesses.

Relationship marketing can help here. For example, in the small business market for certain types of office equipment (eg facsimile, copiers, personal computers and telephones), the direct response advertisement and the catalogue, coordinated through the customer database, is becoming the industry standard for reaching the customer. Once the prospect has become a customer, relationship marketing can be used to maintain the dialogue, while supplies and upgrades are bought, until the equipment needs replacing.

Relationship marketing provides an ideal way of building loyalty and maximising revenue. For example, the quality of customer service may be checked by a questionnaire to all customers. This could monitor customer satisfaction and intention to purchase next time. The results of the questionnaire could be used to identify problems and ensure that dissatisfied customers do not become ex-customers. Such a question- naire could also be used to structure campaigns aimed at managing the replacement cycle. Mailings could be sent just after purchase, half way through the expected life of the product, and close to replacement decision time.

Alternative sales channels

Many businesses find that their ability to serve their customers needs is constrained by the cost of accessing them – the cost of the sale – and are turning to relationship marketing to solve this supply problem. As we saw above, if you are in this situation, relationship marketing can lower your cost of sales, through applications such as telemarketing, mail order, enquiry management, and the like. In some industries, mail order has taken over many of the traditional functions of the sales representative, eg the insurance industry. Customer information centres are used to reduce costs of handling enquiries and to enable sales offices to focus on the next stage of the sale. Idle enquirers and less interested customers are screened out and given other treatment, ensuring that they remain satisfied without incurring the cost of a sales call. In all these examples, the key to success is to match the cost of sales with the actual or potential value of the customer.

Barriers to market entry

Businesses may find themselves unable to enter a market, when faced with competitors who hold a high quality customer database that is used effectively. In some cases, this database can be a unique asset. The cost of setting up such a database may make entry difficult or impossible for other contenders. Conversely, possession of a relationship marketing capability may be the key to entering new markets.

New products and services

Information is increasingly being regarded as a product to be sold in its own right. Relationship marketing is by itself creating new products and services. This new information market is in early stages of development. Strategic alliances between database marketers are beginning to be formed. Banks, automobile manufacturers, financial services companies, and publishers are planning new joint venture businesses, pooling the data that each possesses to build a comprehensive picture of their customers.

QUANTIFYING RELATIONSHIP MARKETING

In competitive strategy formulation, relationship marketing is most frequently used to achieve one or both of the following objectives:

❑ Revenue defence and development.
❑ Cost reduction.

Many of the opportunities opened up by relationship marketing affect both costs and revenue. Some lead to increased revenue while costs stay static or rise more slowly than revenue. Others lead to falling costs while revenue stays static or falls more slowly than costs. These effects will be achieved by the development and implementation of particular *applications* of relationship marketing, such as telemarketing.

Many of the changes produced have a short- and a long-term dimension. For example, telemarketing may produce cost savings and revenue increases that arise relatively quickly through reducing the cost of contacting and selling to customers and by increasing market coverage. These shorter-term effects are not once and for all, but continue so long as you continue to use the application. However, greater market coverage and reduced cost of coverage may allow you to enter different product markets. You may be able to sell a wider product range to existing customers. You may also be able to sell information resulting from the application.

The revenue and cost changes that might result from different aspects of relationship marketing must therefore be identified and quantified. This can be done in many ways, eg:

❑ By category of customer.
❑ By category of product.
❑ By application introduced (eg salesforce support, inbound or outbound telemarketing, direct mail).
❑ By category of change (ie whether it is cost saving, revenue defence or growth).
❑ By time period (short, medium or long term).
❑ By category of staff, function or marketing channel (eg impact on field salesforce, sales offices, retail outlets, physical distribution, marketing communication, market research).

Cost-reduction and revenue-increasing effects of some changes are inseparable. If more revenue comes from a fixed cost base, costs fall as a proportion of sales.

The quantification process can be carried out as follows.

Target opportunities

Are many of the best ideas already present in your company?

You need to generate a shortlist of target opportunities for managing your customers better. This is usually best achieved in management workshops. This may be supplemented by a series of management interviews and discussions. You may find that many of the best ideas are already present in your company. They may not have been allowed to emerge because of the way in which your policies are planned and implemented. After all, many relationship marketing applications are the implementation of common-sense ideas through the use of modern information technology. They may involve:

❑ Reorganising workflows or changing organisational structure and reporting lines.
❑ Re-engineering processes.
❑ Policy development within existing functions, departments, product groups etc.
❑ Opening up of internal communication channels.
❑ Revenue development opportunities.
❑ Revenue protection ideas.
❑ Quality control measures.

The outcome of this step is a statement of your target opportunities. This provides the focus for the rest of the analysis.

Incremental revenue

Existing marketing plans should be reviewed to identify long-term revenue growth objectives and to clarify the basis for revenue growth plans. Revenue growth plans may be based on factors such as overall market growth, specific marketing strategies (product range, price, distribution, advertising, etc), or anticipated competitive changes. Areas to be considered where an improved relationship will make a difference are:

❑ Improving retention rates by x per cent (even small percentages may have a very large impact on the bottom line).
❑ Cross selling (how many of your customers buy both product A and product B). If this percentage is increased, you can usually make

substantial additional profits, if only by spreading marketing and administrative costs over larger revenues.

❑ Upselling.

❑ Improving renewal rates.

❑ Becoming better at reactivating lapsed customers.

This analysis will indicate the areas where relationship marketing may generate revenue growth through improving the effectiveness of policies that are already planned. Table 4.2 contains some examples of other revenue generation or protection areas.

Cost changes

Quantifying the cost savings from implementing relationship marketing prior to implementation is not easy. It is even more difficult if your existing marketing information is not well organised. If you have only recently adhered to the marketing creed, the information required to quantify cost effects may have to be estimated. This may require not only 'reconstruction of figures', based on estimates of staff, but the use of pilot studies, where particular applications are implemented.

Typically, a comprehensive exercise to gather and analyse cost information is required. It will normally cover every channel of communication and distribution to customers, such as salesforce, sales offices operating by telephone and mail, retail outlets, media advertising, and direct mail. The aim is to quantify costs which may be changed by relationship marketing approaches. This exercise is based on interviews, questionnaires, and analysis of financial and operating information relating to the channels of communication and distribution. This analysis may have to be carried out by market sector and product line as well as for the whole business, as some of the opportunities may be confined to particular products or sectors.

For example, suppose that you need to estimate the cost-reducing effects on a salesforce. The data needed include:

❑ Salesforce activity analysis, to find out how your sales staff are spending their time, in particular, time spent on low productivity activities, such as prospecting and converting low potential customers, compared with time spent on high productivity activities (time spent converting high potential customers or preventing their loss).

❑ Sales revenue productivity statistics, to measure the productivity of the time actually devoted to your customers.

❑ Data on market size (overall and by product – number of customers

Table 4.2   *Revenue defending or increasing opportunities*

Will you achieve the following?

Field sales force and sales office

Higher revenue due to ability of sales staff to concentrate calling on higher revenue prospects

Less lost business and fewer lost customers due to improved customer care, as relationship marketing provides improved channels for customers to signal needs

Enhanced new product revenues due to improved ability to target customers for new products and (eventually) consequently, greater ease of launching new products

Greater ability of salesforce to handle broader product portfolio, due to deployment of response-handling system to inform relevant customers prior to the sales call

Market research

Greater ability to identify potential for increased revenue among existing customers

Business and marketing planning

More coherent plans to address new revenue opportunities, due to higher quality and relevance of information, leading to higher success rate with launch of new products, greater matching of distribution channels to customer needs, etc

Retail

Ability to market additional products to existing retail customers, whether at retail or through mail order, due to quality of customer information

Higher sales volumes of existing products due to ability to target promotions

Marketing communications

Greater effectiveness of communicating with customers and prospects, leading to higher revenue for given cost

Product marketing

Reduced costs of selling, due to better attunement of channels to customer needs, leading to ability to capture higher market share through lower prices

Inventory

Lower stock-outs and therefore quicker inflow of revenue and reduced loss of sales to competition due to improved sales forecasting

---

and revenue potential), to enable you to estimate the proportion of the market (overall or for given products) left uncovered by your salesforce.

❑ Data on how the activity profile of your salesforce changes when you implement relationship marketing and put relevant applications (eg telemarketing, direct mail) to work.

❑ Data on the current costs of managing your salesforce.

❑ Information on how the activities which generate these costs affect the productivity of your sales staff.
❑ Information on how relationship marketing disciplines will lead to a change in the nature and scale of these activities (eg data provision work by support staff).

Contact strategies

The current method of contacting customers should be determined. Future contact strategy options, using relationship marketing, should then be identified, and an assessment made of:

❑ The capability of existing channels to support revenue growth targets and the cost of resourcing those channels to achieve them.
❑ The incremental cost of the relationship marketing strategy needed to support the revenue growth target.

With these and other data, cost effects can then be calculated. Consider the business-to-business example in Figure 4.1. Suppose that a field sales visit costs £250, a highly skilled telephone account management call £8 and a mailing £1 per contact, and the spread of contacts throughout the year is as indicated. In the future strategy, the large (not largest) and medium-size accounts account for a cost of sales reduction of up to 64 per cent. In the low volume accounts, although the cost of sales (COS) has been increased, at least we are talking to them, giving them the opportunity to identify themselves as potential purchasers. Notice that in all cases the number of contacts per year has actually increased. Clearly the measure here will be not just cost of sales, but revenue and customer

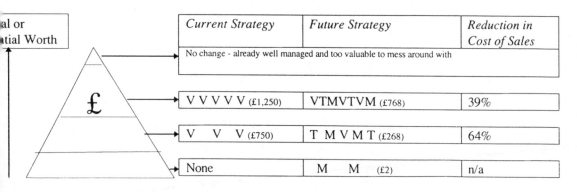

	Current Strategy	Future Strategy	Reduction in Cost of Sales
No change - already well managed and too valuable to mess around with			
	V V V V V (£1,250)	VTMVTVM (£768)	39%
	V V V (£750)	T M V M T (£268)	64%
	None	M M (£2)	n/a

V = sales visit; T = telephone call; M = mail.

Figure 4.1 Calculating the reduction in cost of sales

satisfaction. Some customers will whole-heartedly resist being managed by the telephone. Others will actually welcome it! The key is to identify which ones are which.

Other potential cost reduction areas are illustrated in Table 4.3.

REVENUE AND COST REVIEW

A summary of marketing activity over the period of the plan should then be prepared. This should show the effect on costs and revenues of employing existing methods to achieve targets, and compare it with the costs and revenues implied by the use of relationship marketing. This should show the areas where relationship marketing is more effective.

If the analysis indicates the need for distribution channel change underpinned by relationship marketing, the result might be a wholesale change in the revenue/cost profile. Whole categories of cost may disappear (eg the abolition of sales branches) and new ones appear (eg their replacement by a central sales coordination unit). Distribution channel change may create further strategic marketing opportunities, such as the ability to address whole new markets or launch completely different types of product. However, the change may be less revolutionary, eg the refocusing of a calling salesforce on larger customers and the support or replacement of their efforts by a telemarketing operation.

Relationship marketing may afford many opportunities for increasing revenue and reducing costs, but unless these opportunities are firmly built into operating plans as targets, they are unlikely to be achieved. There needs to be agreement with the appropriate revenue- or cost-responsible functions concerning how revenue and cost opportunities are to be captured. It is therefore important for these functions to be involved in the whole strategic appraisal process.

HOW MUCH TO SPEND

Here, the answer is surprisingly simple. It is:

As much as is profitable.

Your research should show you what you risk when relationship marketing fails, and what you gain when you get it right. It will also show where problems are greatest and where pay-off is likely to be highest. It will also show what problems are faced by customers and what needs to be done to resolve them. The next step is the financial calculation – how much extra profit you will make. In some cases, the calculation may look

Table 4.3   *Potential areas of cost reduction*

Will you achieve any of the following?

Field salesforce

Reduction in number needed for given market coverage. This would be through a more efficient calling pattern and less time spent identifying prospects and obtaining prospect information

Reduced staff support required, due to higher quality information available to sales staff

Reduced systems support, due to unification of possible variety of support systems

Reduced salesforce turnover due to quality of support and consequent higher motivation

Possibly broader span of management control and reduced number of reporting levels feasible. This would be due to a better standard of information on activities and effectiveness of field sales staff, leading to lower management costs

Sales office

Reduced number of staff required to deal with a given number of customers or support a given number of field sales staff. This would be due to reduction in time spent obtaining and collating information and more efficient prospecting systems

Reduced costs of handling customer enquiries due to improved structuring of response handling mechanism, so that customer enquiries go to relevant destination more smoothly without passing through irrelevant hands

Lower staff turnover due to higher level of support, and consequent improved morale

Broader span of control and reduced number of reporting levels feasible, due to better standard of information on activities and effectiveness of office sales staff, leading to lower management costs

Reduction in number of branch offices due to ability to cover market better and more 'remotely'

Market research

Lower expenditure on external research, due to higher quality and relevance of information available on customers and prospects

Marketing and business planning

Reduced costs of information collection and management, due to availability of higher quality, more relevant and updated information on customers and prospects, leading to possible reduction in numbers of planning staff or in planning component of other jobs

Retail

Improved site planning, due to ability to match customer profiles to area profiles more accurately. This might lead to a reduction in the number of outlets to attain given revenue targets

Lower surplus inventory, due to ability to target 'sale' merchandise marketing

Higher utilisation of space, due to ability to market special in-store events to database

Product/brand marketing

Reduced costs of selling, due to better attunement of existing and new channels – some of which are only possible using relationship marketing – to customer needs

Marketing communications

Lower costs for achieving any given task, due to greater accountability and to improved ability to identify targets for communication and make communication relevant and therefore more effective

Inventory

Reduced write-offs due to reduced frequency of launch of inappropriate products and to earlier termination of dying products

General improved forecastability of marketing campaigns, leading to reduced temporary inventory peaks for given products one sided, because you may be forced to improve relationship marketing just to meet competitive standards and stay in business. So include revenue protection.

Because of interdependence between different relationship marketing activities, and the expectation customers may have for continuous improvement, it may be best to develop a long-term programme of improvement, with recalibration at intervals. This serves to check how customer needs have changed in the interim and to monitor the effectiveness of implementation of your actions.

NEW OPPORTUNITIES FOR IMPROVING RELATIONSHIP MARKETING

This section should probably be called 'new necessities for improving relationship marketing', at least in competitive markets. This is because low management awareness of the link between relationship marketing, profit and competitiveness implies a poor outlook for companies whose relationship marketing standards fall behind those of the competition.

Management awareness that there is a close connection between relationship marketing and profit and that the strength of this connection can be quantified can lead to new approaches to customer management, starting with the identification of groups of customers who wish to be managed differently, and ending with a long-term commitment to achieving differentiated and higher levels of relationship marketing in order to maximise profit. The essence of the new approach is a much stronger customer orientation in business and marketing strategy.

FEASIBILITY ANALYSIS

Two constraints which warrant further research are:

1. Technical feasibility.
2. Financial/resource feasibility.

Technical feasibility

Technical feasibility is defined as levels (frequency, type and quality of contact, planned outcomes) of relationship marketing that it is possible to deliver, at different resource levels. Here, levels of relationship marketing should be translated into likely resulting customer behaviour, as your next step is to work out what levels of relationship marketing it is worth providing, measured against the rewards to you in terms of changed customer behaviour.

Financial feasibility

Once the alternatives that are achievable through relationship marketing actions are identified, you are in a position to research financial feasibility.

Relationship marketing is an investment decision like any other, and should therefore be subject to the same financial disciplines. This should ensure the provision of the right relationship level. It is possible to over-invest in the relationship, with no real return. Assessing financial feasibility requires quantifying the costs of relationship marketing policies and setting them against the benefits (eg reduced future costs of query handling, increased profit through increased sales). This is not always a question of simple calculations. You may have to make assumptions about financial and market factors that will apply in the future. You will also have to make assumptions about:

❑ How customer needs will evolve.
❑ What products customers are likely to buy.
❑ What future costs of provision of relationship marketing are likely to be.

Relationship marketing sounds very nice to the marketer, but red lights may flash for your financial management when this term is used, for it can be a bottomless pit for hard-earned money. Hence the need to justify all relationship marketing expenditure in terms of your financial objectives. The best justification for you is increased business from existing customers, reduction in customer losses and more new customers.

The best justification is increased business from existing customers, reduction in customer losses and more new customers.

Relationship marketing does not come in large indivisible packages. Advocates of increased investment in relationship marketing should be asked to justify not only the whole package but every individual element of it. This is the only way to stop the building in of unnecessary costs.

The main areas of cost in setting up relationship marketing include:

❑ Systems (hardware, software development and/or licences, telecommunications).
❑ Training (including time off territory for sales staff).
❑ Culture shift education programmes for the organisation.
❑ Process re-engineering.

❏ Policy development (time).
❏ Setting up of new units (eg telemarketing units).
❏ Closure of old units (eg branches).
❏ Redundancy payments.

These must be set against the marketing benefits. These lie principally in the areas of customer acquisition and retention. Your ability to acquire and retain customers depends critically on how well you satisfy their needs – the subject of the next chapter.

Chapter 5
Identifying Customer Relationship Needs

THE TEN KEY QUESTIONS

The key questions you face in deciding what approach to take in relationship marketing are:

1. With which customers do you want to create and manage a relationship?
2. What are these customers' behaviours, needs and perceptions?
3. What is their relative importance, eg do they constitute a hierarchy?
4. How far do your policies and operations meet their needs today?
5. What are relevant competitive offerings against which you should position yours?
6. What are your customers' experiences of your products, services and of the relationship as a whole?
7. What do your staff believe about their role in your relationship with customers?
8. What do commercial indicators of relationship success show (eg brand loyalty, market share)?
9. Can your customers be grouped into coherent segments, to enable relationship marketing policy to be structured to meet their needs?
10. What are these segments, and are they stable?

THE RESEARCH PROCESS AND THE POLICY PROCESS

Clearly, many of the answers should be sought from customers. You can't build a relationship without talking to the other party first! The *research* process should be integrated closely with the *policy* process.

Information is not being gathered for the sake of it, but to influence policy. This means that the content, coverage and timing of research should be integrated within the planning process. To ensure this, each piece of research should:

- ❏ **Have specific objectives.**
- ❏ **Improve the quality of the next piece of research.**
- ❏ **Have clear policy outcomes.**

WHAT IS 'THE POLICY PROCESS'?

The conventional policy process works for relationship marketing just as well as for any other area of decision making. This process consists of:

1. Research and analysis – to identify what is possible and what customers need. This should cover the product and service portfolio, relationship standards and customer behaviour.
2. Determination of objectives, policies and main projects – to ensure that the policies required to meet customer needs are adopted.
3. Agreement on the details of policies and implementation projects – to ensure delivery of the policies.
4. Measurement and control – to ensure that your policies are properly implemented and the need for any modifications picked up.

This policy process must include:

1. How your relationship marketing will cause it to stand out from that offered by other suppliers – whether directly or indirectly competitive, or suppliers whose standards of relationship marketing are likely to provide a basis for comparison. This answers the question 'How well should you be perceived to be performing, when compared to other suppliers?' This is defined as *competitiveness*.
2. What should be done to ensure that your customer needs are met, ie the answer to the questions 'What does the customer want to happen in their relationship with you?' and 'What do you want to happen so that these customer needs are met?'. These are defined as *relationship performance requirements*.

RESEARCHING COMPETITIVE REQUIREMENTS

Competitive relationship marketing performance must be researched and assessed. This immediately raises the question as to whom should be regarded as competition. The answer to this lies mainly with customers, who have their own basis for comparison, so it is enough to ask them.

Where direct competitors are absent or are not very large or effective, consumers may choose 'parallel' organisations – those they see as involved in similar activities, or as similarly large. Thus, telecommunications may be compared with other utilities – gas, water and electricity. However, utilities may be compared to retailers, as the latter provide most consumers with their commonest experience of interaction with large commercial organisations.

As usual, we need to distinguish between:

❑ What relationship marketing competitors *are* delivering.
❑ What customers *perceive* them to be delivering.

What's being delivered today

Customers' perceptions about what is being delivered are, of course, determined partly by what your competitors actually deliver. This in turn is partly determined by the policies they have in place to deliver it. Obviously, it is not always possible to get detailed information on competitive policies. Strategies for doing this include:

---

1. Direct (formal or informal) exchange of information with competitors. This is most feasible when:
   – competition is indirect;
   – relationship marketing is not seen by their top management as a major factor in overall competitive success;
   – competitors have to work together on specific customer projects (eg as industrial equipment suppliers often have to).
2. Hiring competitive staff.
3. Briefing market research agencies to collect data. This can be done through:
   – agencies interviewing competitive staff;
   – using agencies to set up 'multi-client studies', in which competitors pool information on an anonymous basis.
4. Experiencing relationship marketing – by becoming a customer of the company concerned.

Particular issues to examine are:

1. How reliable is the delivery of relationship marketing – is it variable in quality, timing etc?
2. What channels or media are used to manage the customer?
3. What does the delivery depend upon? Is it led by systems, processes, or simply personal initiative of their staff?
4. How much does it cost to deliver it? This may need to be based on informed guesses about the kinds of policies, procedures, and resources that are being used to deliver relationship marketing.

5. What benefits does the competitor derive from it? Information on this may be derived from market research on customer loyalty.

The competitive future

Researching the current competitive position is not enough. Relying solely on today's information would lead to relationship marketing policies designed to meet past requirements and situations. Therefore, you need to:

❑ Examine past trends in competitive policies.
❑ Try to assess how your competitors are thinking about this area.
❑ Examine any information you have about their recruitment of staff, or suppliers likely to be involved in developing relationship marketing.

RELATIONSHIP PERFORMANCE REQUIREMENTS

The most important activity in researching customer relationship needs is to define customers' general perceptions, wants, and expectations regarding the relationship. This means finding answers to the questions in Table 5.1.

The information in the table relates to what customers need in the way of relationship. To this must be added information on:

1. What relationship is actually achieved (as perceived by customer and supplier).
2. What changes are planned in relationship management.

The result of the above analysis should be a comparison between current and planned levels of relationship management and customer needs. This will be fed into the next stage of the process.

The contact audit

You need to understand how the different contacts a customer has with you affect customers' attitudes and perceptions concerning the relationship. The contact audit begins identifying all the contact points. The audit shows the type, nature, frequency, and quality of contact with customers. It should also show how these contacts affect customers'

Table 5.1 *Relationship performance requirements*

Which performance requirements do you know now or need to research?	Know now	Research
1. What are the principal dimensions which customers use to measure relationship performance, eg information exchanged, long- and short-term benefits of the relationship, contact frequency, speed of query or complaint resolution, staff behaviour?		
2. How do customers perceive current levels of performance?		
3. When do customers believe that the relationship starts, and within it transactions and contact episodes?		
4. What are the minimum levels of relationship achievement that customers will tolerate while staying loyal?		
5. What is the maximum level of relationship management that customers believe that it would be reasonable for you to supply?		
6. What are the main areas where customers see the need for improvement?		
7. How strongly do customers feel about relationship performance?		
8. How important is the relationship in customers' decisions to buy the core product or service?		
9. Where does the customer wish the locus of control of the relationship to be?		
10. What changes in all the above are likely to occur during the period for which policy is being made? What will cause these changes (eg economic, social or demographic factors, competitive actions)?		
11. What image of you would the customer like to have?		
12. Is it possible to identify particular groups of customers with significantly different relationship requirements?		
13. If there is a risk of certain types of customer not being 'right' for you in some way, what reasons for your refusing to do business with them will be accepted by these customers?		

perceptions and attitudes. You may be surprised, as many managers are, to find how many points of contact exist between your organisation and your customers.

You may be surprised to find how many points of contact exist between you and your customers.

MAKING SENSE OF CUSTOMER DATA

Except in the smallest organisation, relationship marketing policies cannot be completely tailored to the needs of individual customers. If you have very high quality information about customers, do not mistake the ability to identify differences in relationship needs at the individual level for the ability to deliver different relationships. You will almost certainly need to group customers. The most relevant way to group them is according to their attitudes and likely responses to relationship marketing policies.

The importance of segmentation

Segmentation is just another word for putting customers into groups that share similar characteristics that affect their behaviour in the market (buying, media etc). Segmentation is used because:

1. It gives you a better basis for understanding the whole market. Even if you market the same product or service to segments which behave differently, you will understand the whole market better if you know how different segments behave. However, if the relationship is an important part of a complex product/service offering, then it is possible to adjust the relationship to different types of customer, while making the same core offer.
2. If different segments respond differently to marketing policy, and if policies can be attuned to different segments, you can achieve your objectives more easily than if you follow an undifferentiated policy (ie applied to the whole market). If the relationship needs of different kinds of customer differ quite radically, then the total product/service offering may be differentiated purely or mainly in terms of the relationship offered.
3. Segmentation can bring benefits of focus, concentration and specialisation and hence differentiation. These benefits include increased profit or sales, lower costs and prevention of competitive entry. This is because a focused marketing policy makes you very good at meeting the needs of your chosen segment(s). If the relationship needs of each segment are analysed in depth, you are in a strong position to fine-tune your relationship offering so as to meet the needs of your chosen segment.

Relationship marketing policies can be anything from very general, ie applicable to the whole market, or highly differentiated, with different procedures being followed for different kinds of customers and situations. If you want to meet the needs of many different types of customer, you can opt for a core relationship offering, with 'add-ons' targeted at specific segments.

Taking the customer into account

The above analysis shows that your customers cannot be treated as just one-dimensional objects. They are a complex mix of personality, motivations, attitudes and needs, who prefer particular kinds of experiences and learn from them. Relationship marketing policy must take this into account. Obviously, you cannot understand every customer in such depth. But you must understand the customer's perspective in order to be able to meet customer needs.

The demand for attention

Customers have some idea of the kind and level of relationship they want or do not want. Between neglect and an over-attentive relationship lies a wide range of possibilities. How can you possibly allow for the wide range of requirements that your customers might have? The answer to this lies in the many different ways in which you can differentiate the relationship. These include:

1. Giving information: about products, services, deliveries, current status of the relationship, how your customers can access you, how they can get more information, different ways of paying, what kinds of relationship they can have with you.
2. Obtaining information about customers' needs: what they need, when, how, etc.
3. Giving commitment to supply.
4. Gaining commitment to buy.
5. Providing reassurance.
6. Helping the customer buy or use, to obtain maximum benefit.
7. Improving service.

PLANNING THE RELATIONSHIP

All customers will have different requirements at different levels. Meeting the right combination of needs is easier the earlier in your business planning process you start your relationship planning. You need to:

1. Decide with which customers a relationship is to be created.
2. Assess researching and modelling needs.
3. Determine the type and level of relationship to be provided, to meet customer needs and supplier objectives.
4. Build flexibility into your relationship delivery system so you can meet individual variations within general requirements.

CHOOSING CUSTOMERS

Not every supplier has the luxury of being able to choose customers. For example, public utilities and retailers must normally do business with any customer, no matter how problematic or litigious. But the issue is not simply one of what customers can do in principle. Rather, it is a question of which of these customers are most encouraged to buy. By branding, marketing communications, store layout, pricing, product range and all the other items of the marketing mix, particular kinds of customer can be attracted while others can be deterred. For example, retail customers requiring a very close relationship may understand from the layout and staffing of a self-service store and the absence of any loyalty or storecard scheme that they are unlikely to get their required relationship. In an upmarket fashion department store, the layout and numbers of assistants and the existence of a combined storecard and loyalty scheme gives a different message.

A key principle of relationship marketing is that it is hard to meet all your customers' needs all of the time. It is therefore essential to prioritise customers and needs. Competitive survival requires meeting the most important needs of the most important customers. Competitive advantage is obtained by doing this – and meeting the needs of customers whose needs are not being met by competitive providers.

For this reason, you must:

❑ Have a good understanding of the needs of different groups of customers.
❑ Prioritise customers and needs.

But there is a prior decision – with which groups of customer a relationship should be created.

THE IDEA OF STRATEGIC SEGMENTATION

You should find the following hierarchy of segmentation helpful in targeting.

Analytical segmentation

Here, you analyse customer and market information to identify that you do have different groups of customers with different profiles, needs, etc. You start with very broad questions such as 'What kinds of customer do I have, what is their behaviour, which products or channels are the most successful at managing them?' The segments that you identify in this way may never be subjected to different promotions, policies or strategies. For example, you may aggregate them into a target market for a promotion. The main criterion for successful use of analytical segmentation is that any resulting strategies work overall, because they are based on in-depth understanding of customer needs. Analytical segmentation often provides the foundation for the other three types of segmentation.

Response segmentation

Here, you identify different groups of customers for targeting particular promotions. A given customer may belong to a whole series of different segments, according to the objectives of individual promotions. The key success criterion for response segmentation is the success of each of your promotions (ie whether your response rates met expectations, whether final purchases hit your targets).

Strategic segmentation

Here, you identify groups of customers who need to be handled differently in some way. For example, mass-market financial services suppliers need to identify:

❑ Loan customers who are likely to be higher credit risks (in which case they are usually only accepted as borrowers at an interest rate which covers the risk premium).

❑ Mortgage customers who are likely to be rapid switchers, in which case they may only be accepted for loans with higher penalties for earlier cancellation.

Conversely, low risk or infrequently-switching customers will be targeted and marketed to intensively, and particular attention might be paid to the quality of the relationship established with them.

The idea of strategic segmentation is to ensure that each of your actual or potential customers is allocated, at a minimum, to at least one strategic category, membership of which carries certain implications for your marketing policy towards them. You must avoid creating too many categories, with attendant risks of both overlap (a given customer being subjected to too many marketing initiatives or restrictions, which have to be resolved by prioritisation rules) and of over-complexity (because of the number of segments that need to be addressed with different marketing policies). An issue of particular importance for strategic segmentation is the movement of customers between categories.

Delivered loyalty segmentation

This is a special case of strategic segmentation. Here, you identify particular groups of actual or potential customers whose loyalty is critical to you. This criticality normally relates to the volume and profitability of business coming from this group of customers, but may also be related to other variables (eg political sensitivity). Identification of this group is followed by the development *and* implementation (or 'delivery') of a practical marketing approach, including branding, relationship management (through whichever channels are appropriate), promotional management and systems support, which works to draw that group of customers into a special, long-standing, mutually committed and transcending relationship with you. The components of delivered loyalty segmentation are usually no different from ordinary loyalty programmes.

What is different is the *focus of your organisation* upon the segment and commitment of resources to managing the segment profitably and well. Perhaps the most important feature of such segmentation is the degree of commitment of the organisation to the segment. This means that *your organisation must have fully bought-in to the segmentation approach*.

The systems and management characteristics of these four kinds of segmentation are summarised in Table 5.2.

Table 5.2   *Characteristics of segmentation types*

	Analytical	**Response**	**Strategic**	**Loyalty**
Technical approach	Can be left to expert systems and data-mining approaches	Expert/data mining approaches may be used, but test results are key	In-depth business understanding required to define issue	In-depth business understanding required to define issue
Senior management involvement	Not required, except to ensure that capability exists	Required if promotions are a large share of marketing budget	Important in defining areas of strategic focus	Absolutely critical because of subsequent commitment to comprehensive loyalty management approach
Customer contact implications	Depends on conclusion	Customers experience correctly defined and targeted promotions	Customers may be required to give more information and should find that they are being offered more appropriate products and services	Customers who are loyal or who have the propensity to be so experience more integrated management, whatever the contact point and whatever the product or service

RESEARCHING AND MODELLING NEEDS

Many suppliers make the mistake of amassing large amounts of data on customer needs. This data – not surprisingly – usually shows that:

❑ Customers have a great variety of needs.
❑ These needs influence customers' buying behaviour in all sorts of ways.

It is therefore essential for you to try to develop a model of customer behaviour: how it affects your customers' relationship requirements, and how relationship achievement creates business success. This model is essential if relationship needs are to influence policy.

It is essential to develop a model of customer behaviour.

DETERMINING RELATIONSHIP TYPES AND LEVELS

Once you have identified the broad relationship requirements of your target customers through research, the next step is to determine target levels and types of relationship. You need to decide where on the spectrum of relationship management the customer wishes to be – between neglect and intense relationship.

Given that relationship requirements are dependent on customer types and the needs of the moment, exact positioning of customers will not be possible. You must therefore determine the base level of relationship that should be provided. Variations around this level must be achieved either by contractual variations or by flexibility of relationship delivery. You should determine the base level of relationship on strategic, competitive grounds, as an important component of marketing strategy. Likely variations in requirements should be analysed and grouped, so that meeting them can be done without too complex a process. There should also be frequent feedback from customers about the their perceptions and attitudes towards the relationship. In this way, you will ensure that broad policies are correct and that at the frontline, the right attunement to individual needs is taking place.

Building in flexibility

The larger the organisation, the more difficult it seems to be to remain flexible to customer needs. So you need to allow your staff some flexibility. For example, if a customer telephones to ask for a particular delivery date, the person receiving the call can give a precise response if scheduling information has been provided on-line. If your information systems are not capable of delivering this kind of information, then some leeway may be given to the person receiving the call to reduce the customer's uncertainty about delivery dates, with provision for a later call back to confirm date and time.

Flexibility is a key attribute.

Flexibility is a key attribute of relationship marketing. Even the best planning and information systems cannot deliver the quality of relationship of the highly motivated individual, supported by well-planned processes and systems and operating within clear guidelines.

Using market research wisely

A key aspect of the information systems you use in planning and managing relationship marketing is market research. In the next chapter, we explain the special market research disciplines you need in relationship marketing.

Chapter 6
The Role of Market Research

'If you can't measure it, you can't manage it.' This is one of those nicely turned phrases that sounds so obvious that you might wonder why anyone bothered to say it. Of course, it's not even true – many good managers work by feel and produce better results than their peers who feel exposed without measurement. This is even true of relationship marketing, where a policy of 'staying close to customers', and ensuring that staff do the same, can be just as effective as measurement-driven management.

Yet measurement has its place, particularly in large complex businesses, or ones where it is difficult to gain perspective on how customers feel about the relationship. So how should you go about it?

WHAT ARE YOU TRYING TO MEASURE?

If you're trying to find out whether your customers are happy about their relationship with you, then it makes sense to define the scope of any research as to how a customer might perceive the relationship, as well as what they might feel about it. We suggest this definition:

How customers define and perceive their relationship with you overall and particularly during any period in which those customers believe that they are in a transaction with you.

It is normally easier to measure customers' perceptions just at the point when the relationship with you is consummated: the 'moment of truth'. Yet the reality of most customer relationships is that this moment is

What do your customers think of you?

preceded by a period of anticipated contact and followed by reflection. Their attitude to you is formed over a long period and can change, while other contacts or attempts at contact can be made. Here are some examples:

❑ Dialling a Freephone number and receiving the engaged signal.
❑ Trying to fix an appointment with the bank manager.
❑ Browsing in the car showroom but not talking to the sales person.
❑ Visiting a clothes store and leaving without purchasing anything.

The transaction may be of various kinds: sales, service, payment, information seeking, etc. But whatever it is, our first step in research is to find out what the perceived relationship is and, within it, the perceived transaction period, for different types of customer and relationship.

INTERNAL AND EXTERNAL MEASURES

The larger your company, the harder it is for your management to understand all your customers' needs and perceptions, and the more remote they are likely to be from customer contact staff, though this depends upon the nature of your business, and in particular whether the relationship is delivered through people or equipment (eg self-service, computer).

But whatever the situation, you need both a quantitative and qualitative understanding of customers' relationship perceptions and preferences; from the point of view of your company as a whole and from that of your front-line customer-facing staff. This gives you the basis for complete customer management and understanding. Also, a consistent research and measurement initiative demonstrates management's desire to do more than evangelise.

PART OF THE RELATIONSHIP

Don't keep your customers at arm's length.

If you are planning to base your relationship management decisions on measurement, you need to understand that interaction with customers is not an 'arm's length' exercise, but is often a situation in which you and your customer are closely involved with each other, with customers often doing their part to create or consummate the relationship. So you should focus on both the transactions themselves, on your customers and on their overall relationship with you, including how long the relationship has been established, how well it has gone in the past, and their feelings about the relationship. In particular, you must take into account issues such as:

❑ How customers can become emotionally attached to or irritated by particular transactions within an otherwise good relationship, perhaps as delivered by particular individuals.
❑ How branding, product range and customer loyalty affects customers' perceptions of the relationship and what they will say to you.
❑ How slowly customers' attitudes to the overall relationship – including their loyalty to the company – evolve.
❑ How, when your customers' attitudes do evolve, this changes their attitudes to individual transactions within the relationship, including the slightly paradoxical fact that loyal customers are often the most difficult to manage, because they have higher expectations of the relationship.
❑ Whether customers feel in some way dependent on you, or wish to be strongly in control, and how this might affect what they say about you.

WHAT TECHNIQUES ARE AVAILABLE?

In this brief chapter, we cannot cover all possible techniques in detail. In fact, the techniques are all part of the standard market research repertoire. So here we focus on what you can and can't do with some of the most commonly used techniques. These techniques are listed in Table 6.1.

Table 6.1 *Research techniques*

Which research techniques should you use?	
1.	Desk research
2.	Qualitative groups
3.	Quantitative research
4.	Telephone questionnaires
5.	Mystery shopping
6.	Competitive research
7.	Service level audit
8.	User groups
9.	Customer feedback
10.	Staff research

Desk research

Reports on previous studies of customer needs and how they are met are particularly valuable. They show the variety of customer needs, but also indicate how these needs can be grouped and what sorts of policies have been used to meet them.

Qualitative groups

With this technique, small groups of customers, selected according to a detailed profile, spend an hour or more with an experienced researcher discussing specific relationship and service issues and responding to pre-defined statements. Properly used, ie with participants properly selected, and the discussion conducted by a professional researcher and reported comprehensively, groups will give you a detailed understanding of how a cross-section of customers feel about these issues. They also offer an opportunity to deal with anecdotal evidence in a positive and constructive way. If you are in a hurry to confirm an idea or diagnose a problem, groups probably provide the quickest turnround time, often as little as two to three weeks. An additional benefit is that groups give customers a warm feeling that you really care and want to listen to their views, a feeling that is enhanced by their receiving payment for participation or – better – gifts of your products or services.

However, groups only give you the views of a few people, tens rather than the hundreds or thousands needed for a representative sample. So they won't:

❏ Give you a continuous audit of standards and trends in their achievement.
❏ Provide a benchmark against which to set relationship management standards.

Groups may not be popular with staff if their positive benefits are not sold properly. Researching individual customers is one thing, getting them together to talk about your company and (as staff may see it) their role in it is another, so staff sometimes do resist helping recruit customers.

Quantitative research

This involves running detailed questionnaires on many respondents. Questionnaires are usually structured, ie with carefully formulated questions mostly requiring specific answers, although room may be left for a broader range of responses. In some cases, eg for senior decision makers buying business services, questionnaires may be unstructured, with the interviewer working through a check-list of more open-ended questions. Questionnaire design is usually based on the results of group research, the latter being used to identify the language your customers use in talking about you and the relationship you provide, and their key concerns.

This approach should be used if you want a large enough sample to derive a statistically valid result. If qualitative information is required, this can be elicited through asking consumers more detailed questions about why they respond in particular ways to particular questions. Mail questionnaires have these advantages:

❑ they are more economical and convenient than personal interviews;
❑ they avoid interviewer bias;
❑ they give people time to consider their answers;
❑ they can be anonymous;

and these disadvantages:

❑ the questions need to be very straightforward if the response is to be valid;
❑ answers must be taken as final;
❑ respondents see the whole questionnaire before answering it;
❑ it is impossible to be sure that the right person answers it;
❑ many recipients may not respond;
❑ non-response may lead to bias in results, because those not responding are different in some way from those responding (eg they may be less loyal customers);
❑ the higher the response rate, the more valid the result. But the only way to check this is by chasing up a sample of responders.

Response can be increased by:

❑ Using a covering letter explaining what the survey is doing, how the respondent's name was selected, and why the recipient should reply.
❑ Telling the respondent the benefits of replying.
❑ Explaining why the survey is important.
❑ Enclosing a stamped addressed or business reply envelope.
❑ Giving a premium for responding.
❑ Following up.

If the questionnaire is properly designed and administered to a representative sample of customers regularly, quantitative research will give a detailed and continuing view of:

- ❏ Perceptions: what relationship customers think they are actually in.
- ❏ Satisfaction levels: how satisfied they are with it.
- ❏ Tolerance: what service levels customers will tolerate within the relationship, and what levels they won't.
- ❏ Desires: what customers would really like and, where relevant, what they'd be prepared to sacrifice to obtain it (price, user costs, etc).

Analysis of responses will also show how these are related to each other, and should also provide the key to:

- ❏ Relationship design, when analysed together with customer characteristics and 'grossed-up' to provide a picture of service demand for the whole market.
- ❏ Standard setting.

Research aimed at determining customers' satisfaction levels should aim not only to find out levels of satisfaction, but also causes of variations over time and between branches, individuals, etc.

In service industries, where the research is just required to monitor achievement of relationship management standards, use of self-completion questionnaires, administered by point-of-contact staff, can demonstrate management's trust in these staff and can secure their involvement. However, care must be taken to monitor possible bias because of customers' desire to please or punish the individual staff member who has served them. In some cases, anonymity is also critical. In the best of all worlds, where staff are totally responsible, and where service levels and outcomes are measurable in hard business terms, eg sales and profit, staff can run the system, use the results and relay them to a wider audience. This can lead to a nearly ideal mix of staff involvement, customer satisfaction and profit.

However, questionnaires will not give in-depth views of the emotion that lies behind decisions and complaints.

If your business is one in which customer data is hard to come by, and you are keen to use database marketing techniques, a customer questionnaire is one of the best ways of gathering data – not only on customer attitudes towards the service, but also on the customers themselves and how they use the service. Airlines and car manufacturers are two of the best examples of this use.

Telephone questionnaires

These are used in very similar contexts to mail questionnaires, with the notable addition of questionnaires administered when customers call in to respond to a promotion. Telephone surveys are normally more accurate than mail surveys and combine many of the advantages of mail questionnaires and in-depth interviews, in that:

❑ They are private.
❑ They are one-to-one.
❑ The consumer cannot see the whole questionnaire and so focuses on each question as it comes.
❑ Any problems of understanding can be dealt with.
❑ Careful scripting helps avoid interview bias.
❑ Computerised routing of questionnaires allows for complex patterns of behaviour to be captured.
❑ Response rates are higher – customers can be called until they reply.
❑ Costs are lower than personal interviews.
❑ The telephone is a way of life to business.
❑ Speed: telephones get higher priority than post, and the results are immediately available.

Their disadvantages are that:

❑ Some consumers object to the approach.
❑ The costs of setting up a telephone questionnaire can be high.
❑ Calling costs are higher than postal costs.
❑ It is a voice medium only, so customers' reactions cannot be seen.

In telephone, postal or face-to-face interviewing, there is now much accumulated expertise about how to design questionnaires to elicit relationship marketing needs and attitudes. The recommendations arising from this experience can be summarised as follows:

❑ Do not rely on satisfaction ratings alone. This may give a useful idea of the extent to which customers are satisfied with the relationship, but it does not give a good indication of specific requirements. So questions should be oriented to identifying specific needs.
❑ Customers have many needs, so it is important not to try to condense them into a few simple questions. It is usually a good idea to carry out a few in-depth interviews or group discussions to identify the variety of needs, then to design the questionnaire with as many questions as are needed to cover the variety of needs.
❑ Questions should be as specific as possible. General questions bring imprecise answers, which are not so immediately actionable.
❑ The reliability of answers should be cross-checked, by asking the same question in different ways and possibly by combining postal, telephone, and face-to-face interviewing to check consistency across the different techniques.

❑ If comments are asked for (often at the end of the questionnaire), they should be requests for specific recommendations, eg improvements to particular aspects of particular services. General comments have little value.

Mystery shopping

This is a very popular service research technique, particularly among companies that make their service available through a large number of outlets (their own or dealers) or staff (eg telephone-based). This includes not just true service industries, but also suppliers of manufactured goods where the buyer would not be identifiable by name. It is more difficult to use this technique in industrial goods markets except those served through distributors, because in the former it is normal to ask for customer details before handling problems.

In this technique, external staff pose as customers and then rate the service they receive using a form. The approach should be used only after careful planning and consultation with staff, and with a clear policy output which is known to and understood by staff – whether this be a competition or a service policy improvement. Results should be published as soon as possible after the audit, in a non-confrontational, positive way, with the offer of training and resources to remedy any problems highlighted by the audit. This implies that budget should be set aside for this remedial work (a rough guide is: budget ten times as much for improvement as for research).

Competitive research

This is vital. As we stressed in the last chapter, using relationship marketing competitively requires knowledge of how competitors are treating their customers and also what they are doing to achieve their relationships. Some information on this can be gathered from customers using the techniques mentioned above. But experiencing competitive relationships is vital. This is parallel to the manufacturing practice of buying competitive products and stripping them down, to find out how they are made, how reliable they are and what they can do. To experience the relationship, competitive programmes should be subscribed to, and individual components of the relationship tested (eg calling Helplines for customers). Finally, it is important to try to envisage what competitors' own relationship marketing strategies are likely to be.

Internal audit

This involves auditing the relationship as you deliver it, as opposed to as perceived by customers. In many cases, audit data is reported by staff or automated computer systems, eg time to answer the telephone, percentage of calls connected, percentage of trains/flights arriving on time, percentage of calls/contacts where the customer's relationship with the company is not accurately identified. Auditing may be undertaken prior to other forms of research, to identify the 'reality' customers are faced with, and after standard setting (based on the quantitative research), to determine whether standards are being met. You may wish to incorporate the standard into a customers' charter, in which case you will need to audit frequently.

User groups

These exist mainly in business-to-business markets, particularly for services and products that are very important to customers (eg information technology). They are so important as a source of feedback to suppliers that they are often funded by suppliers. They may also conduct their own surveys of their members. As a general feedback mechanism, they are excellent. Since there is much research to show that some of the most successful products and services – particularly in business-to-business markets – are derived from customers' ideas, they also represent an excellent forum in which to test ideas for new products and services. However, they can represent something of a vested interest, particularly if they are dominated by a few big users, so you should take care to ensure representativeness. Where this is difficult, it may be better to sponsor the formation of separate associations, or at least separate sections of the main association.

Customer feedback

This was once the most neglected form of research. It was often treated as 'complaints'. The information arising from complaints was used to rectify the situation the customer was complaining about. Perhaps letters with compliments were passed to the appropriate staff. But the rest of the information was lost. This led to a vicious circle. Customers viewed giving feedback as pointless, since they received no acknowledgement and saw no results in company policy. Staff failed to pass feedback on. This was because:

❑ They saw no actions resulting from their efforts.
❑ The 'shoot the messenger' syndrome was present.

An additional point to bear in mind is that customer behaviour lags behind changes in levels of satisfaction/emotion. For example, a customer who has for many years been satisfied with the relationship with a particular supplier will go on buying from that customer for a time after the relationship starts to deteriorate, and may not complain for some time. Or they may complain immediately, but not become disloyal, so their complaint may be ignored because 'they'll stick with us anyway', or 'they weren't really serious'. Conversely, when matters improve, it may take time for customers to experience the improvement. So they may not return or increase their purchasing/loyalty for some time. This can lead staff to become indifferent about customer feedback, as they do not see the immediate effect of it in company performance.

Use customer complaints positively.

However, today, many large companies realise that improving the relationship provides good long-term benefits. They are deploying a variety of techniques to channel customer feedback into points where it can be dealt with quickly and effectively *and* used to produce information to steer policy.

Positive handling of your customers' complaints wins points with customers and might encourage them to recommend you: sometimes even more than if you had satisfied them in the first instance! This may be because it's only when they complain that you give them attention: a dangerous situation. But using complaints – and other customer-originated comments such as suggestions for improvements – as a measurement is not advisable unless you have left no stone unturned in ensuring that your customers can express their feelings to you when they want to. For there is much research to show that the vast majority of customers don't express their feelings voluntarily to suppliers. Most customers who wish to complain will complain to their friends and colleagues, possibly dissuading them from using the service. Only very satisfied or loyal customers will take the time to write or call. Table 6.2 contains some very effective examples of techniques used to overcome these barriers to customer feedback.

Table 6.2 *Effective techniques to overcome barriers to customer feedback*

Which of these techniques would work for you?

Distributing feedback forms (*note*: not complaint forms), giving customers an incentive to complete them and staff an incentive to ensure that they are completed (eg during service provision, at payment time)

Incorporating feedback routines into other documentation routines (eg delivery notes, receipts, boarding documents, club membership mailings)

Setting up an inbound telemarketing facility to handle calls and promoting the number widely

Calling customers after they have received service

The more you can pre-structure feedback using these techniques, the easier it is for you to analyse, and the greater your opportunity of collecting other data from your customers at the same time.

If your company is very large, the volume of customer feedback may be large enough to justify setting up a specialist customer relations department to handle feedback. In such cases, classification of feedback into different categories can provide useful evidence of the company's success in meeting customer requirements.

Complaints and compliments are very destructive if they are used by themselves to reward or punish staff, as they can obviously be manipulated: customers may find they are put under pressure to 'accentuate the positive and eliminate the negative'. The key here is also to separate the complaint from the complainer, and satisfy the complainer while recording the complaint and dealing with the root cause.

Staff research

If your relationship with customers depends on your staff, the latter's attitudes and opinions should also be researched. This is usually done using questionnaires and focus groups, as with consumers. The aim is to uncover the real truth about the front line. Front-line staff face both ways, and staff workshops will quickly reveal what barriers they face in improving the relationship with your customers. They will also reveal if what you are trying to do is inconsistent with the prevalent culture (eg if you're trying to improve customer loyalty, you need to ensure that staff themselves are loyal and understand the importance of loyalty). If staff turnover is high, you need very strong incentives and people-management processes to get staff to focus on longer-term management of customers, but if your sole objective is to serve customers quickly, the effect of high staff turnover can be managed.

Don't be surprised if staff tell you in workshops that most of the problems lie with the way you've designed their jobs, recruited, trained and managed them. They'll be right: probably because you haven't designed good customer management processes. The workshops will also reveal where staff need new ideas, where they need training, improved communication, and coaching on how to use their existing skills better. They will also reveal where you've recruited the wrong type of people.

In conducting staff research, you need to take into account the views of local management. Many on-site managers are problem-solvers, diving in to sort out problems, then jumping out to sort out problems elsewhere, even thriving on crisis: it makes them feel wanted. The vision you're painting is one in which things run smoothly: they may not like this and resist the whole process of taking staff opinion into account. However, line managers' roles can be structured much better if you design your customer management processes and staff roles around managing customers, put measurement and systems in place to spot problems early, and get managers to deal with the cause rather than the outcome (a fundamental quality principle).

USING THE RESULTS

As with all market research, it is important to allocate the time and money to digest the findings, identify policy conclusions, and implement them. You need to ensure that staff are involved in this process, just as they should be involved in the research. One approach in larger companies is to use review boards, composed of local staff, who review 'their' results against those of other branches, and derive their own conclusions.

INTERPRETING THE RESULTS

Interpreting relationship management research is not always straight-forward. For example, customers who are satisfied when they transact with you won't necessarily rebuy, because satisfaction with the relationship measures only one issue. For example, it ignores the intrinsic quality of the product. So research should always include an element that allows analysis of the connection between attitudes towards the relationship and customers' buying behaviour. Only when this has been done is it advisable to set standards.

COMPETITIVE STANDARDS

Standards should also take into account any relevant competitive benchmarks, so attitudes to relationships with competitive companies should also have been measured. As we stressed in the last chapter, a precondition for this is determining which companies are considered *by customers* to be relevant competitors, and in which respects.

It is also as well to bear in mind what a reasonable standard should be, for it is no use setting unattainable standards, even if they are based on research, as this would be very demotivating for staff. The appropriate policy is therefore to raise standards slowly, as the policies designed to achieve these improvements are implemented. Don't expect that just by setting higher standards you'll achieve long-term improvement: what you'll get is a short-term boost to performance, possibly followed by an increase in staff attrition rates.

So, pacing your improvement is vital. We suggest that if your research shows you're behind your competitors, you should identify the most serious areas of weakness and focus on them, gradually bringing your performance up to par with them. Once you're there, you can focus on getting ahead. The only exception to this is if you believe that a complete re-engineering of how you manage customer relationships will allow you to leap-frog your competitors.

As your business will continue to serve its customers, it should also continue to research them. The culture of listening to customers will only take root if your staff at all levels are involved in the process of listening, interpreting, and then making the changes customers require.

Is it worth researching?

The answer to this question depends on what you're going to do with the research. Normally, the answer is 'only if you're going to manage and improve relationships with customers', and this in turn depends upon the corporate benefit. In competitive markets, asking the question may be unnecessary, as failure to focus through measurement may cause general failure with customers.

Responding to measurement requires management of budgets, over-time, staff turnover (the loyalty culture), revenue and loyalty schemes and, where the relationship is delivered through automated or semi-automated approaches, reconsideration of systems strategies. If you are not prepared to respond fully, then a full measurement programme may not be appropriate. But you may need to do the full measurement at least once to demonstrate to senior management the effects of good customer relationship marketing.

Integrating the research

All the above information sources should be integrated with the results of other kinds of feedback from customers. Staff feedback should also be used, as it is critical to get staff views on what is happening to the

Chapter 7
Customer Retention and Loyalty

STRATEGIC RELATIONSHIP MARKETING

Relationship marketing has often been labelled as an operational tactic, because many of its disciplines derive from direct marketing and, even more specifically, from direct mail.

Its use at the business and indeed corporate level of strategy planning is relatively new, and as yet not universally accepted. The key aspect of relationship marketing is the ability to collect, analyse, and track customer information. This information on your database is a corporate planning asset. Many companies are bought and sold on the knowledge they contain. On balance sheets this is shown as 'goodwill' values, but in relationship marketing terms it is an asset of tangible value: the name and address and all transactional and promotional information on all customers. The lifetime value of customers is yet to appear on balance sheets but it will be an inevitable consequence of a better understanding of relationship marketing.

Collect, analyse and track customer information.

Relationship marketing permeates all levels of strategic planning. At the level of corporate strategy, enhanced customer knowledge means that you can enter new markets with greater degrees of certainty. It can also identify customers under competitive threat and take steps to reinforce their loyalty. At the level of business strategy, relationship marketing provides greater knowledge of particular markets. You can analyse your database to identify specific market and product range opportunities. At the functional level, these same techniques can be used to derive and test product specifications, customer service approaches, and promotional options.

PRINCIPLES OF ACQUISITION AND RETENTION

All objectives and strategies in relationship marketing are based on the concept of customer acquisition and retention. However good you are at devising retention programmes to retain existing customers, there will always be attrition, or loss of customers. In order to stand still, you need to acquire more customers. This is the purpose of an acquisition programme.

ACQUISITION VERSUS RETENTION

Focus on existing customers.

All company sales are made up from two groups, new customers and repeat customers. It is infinitely more cost effective to retain existing customers than attract new customers. Existing customers have identifiable needs that have been satisfied by your products or services. By focusing your marketing strategy on the profitable segments of your customer base, you will normally produce most of the required revenue and increase market share without investing in new customers. Acquisition strategies are much more expensive than retention strategies. If they succeed, the maintenance of customer loyalty has additional benefits. In this book, our focus is clearly on customer retention. 'Loyal' customers not only repurchase, but advocate products and services to their friends, pay less attention to competitive brands and often buy product/service line extensions.

Customer loyalty is not merely created by cross-selling strategies or customer clubs. To develop effective retention strategies, you need a thorough understanding of your customers' behaviour and needs. Loyalty is a physical and emotional commitment given by a customer in exchange for their needs being met. You should view your relationship with customers from their viewpoint. This should help you understand why you are getting your current level of loyalty. As shown in Chapters 5 and 6, research of your existing customers is a key contributor to planning retention.

Customer satisfaction and retention

What customers seek is usually as indicated in Table 7.1. Using information on the customer database, there is no reason why a customer loyalty programme cannot be finely tuned to meet customer relationship needs.

Table 7.1 *Customer satisfaction and retention*

Can you honestly say that you offer all groups of your customers the following?

Convenience and easy access to the right person in the company, first time

Appropriate contact from you and communication from your company

'Special' privileged status as a known customer

Recognition of their history with you

Effective and fast problem solving

Appropriate anticipation of their needs

A professional, friendly, two-way dialogue

WHAT IS CUSTOMER LOYALTY?

Managing customer loyalty is a critical component of relationship marketing. In many companies; the question 'What can we do to increase customer loyalty?' is a recurring theme at board level. Many large companies have joined the select band of companies with tried and tested schemes, while many others are experimenting. Consumer exposure to invitations to join this or that club must have reached an all-time high. But loyalty is not about throwing money into marketing programmes, producing magazines, setting up clubs or introducing cards, in the vague hope that loyalty is generated. Loyalty will be developed over time if the parameters for the relationship are planned and implemented correctly.

But what is 'loyalty'? Loyalty is best defined as a state of mind, a set of attitudes, beliefs, desires, etc. You benefit from customers' loyal *behaviour*, but this results from their state of mind. Loyalty is also a *relative* state of mind. It precludes loyalty to some other suppliers, but not all of them, as a customer could be loyal to more than one competing supplier.

Table 7.2 gives some examples of the difference between state of mind and behaviour. A few points stand out in Table 7.2.

No necessary conditions for loyalty

Not one of the attitudes, beliefs or behaviours is by itself a necessary condition for loyalty to exist. Loyalty is a composite, as is loyal behaviour. Some of the elements of the composition can be very trivial indeed – to you – but not to your customer.

Here are some examples of apparently disloyal behaviour of loyal customers. A loyal customer:

❑ when coming up to a major purchasing decision, may solicit more information from competitive suppliers, for reasons that may include justifying the decision, benchmarking, following formal purchasing processes, or developing a stronger negotiating position;

❑ may buy from competitors if you do not have the right product or service, to avoid risk of dependence, or if you have temporary quality problems.

Table 7.2 *Loyalty state of mind and behaviour*

Loyal attitudes, beliefs and desires	Behaviours
I trust you more than I trust your competitors	Buying from you
I understand you more than I understand your competitors	Buying more from you
I feel at home with you more than with your competitors	Buying exclusively from you
You understand me better than your competitors	Terminating other supply arrangements
I want to learn more about you, but I don't really want to learn more about your competitors	Checking product availability first with you
I want to tell you more about me, but I don't want to tell your competitors	Asking you for information
I want to know what you can do for me, but I don't want to know what your competitors can do	Paying attention to your information (through media, face-to-face, etc)
I want to buy more from you than from your competitors (or more strongly, I don't want to buy from anybody but you)	Giving you information on their characteristics and needs
When I have problems with your products, I know I ought to let you know, but I don't bother with your competitors	Dedicating resources to managing the relationship with you
I believe that you'll deal with these problems well, but I'm not so sure about your competitors	Joining your club
I believe you treat me specially because I am a good customer of yours	Telling you they're a club member, whenever appropriate
	Carrying the symbol (eg card) of your club with them
	Responding more strongly to your incentives, promotions etc
	Recommending or even publicly advocating you to other potential customers
	Notifying problems to you
	Notifying successes to you
	Paying you in time
	Adjusting their buying/usage procedures to fit yours
	Routinising re-ordering from you

Degrees of loyalty

There are also degrees of loyalty. Some customers are very loyal, some less so. Loyalty is therefore developed by approaches that reinforce and develop a positive state of mind and the associated behaviours. The aim is not to make all customers loyal, but rather to improve the loyalty of those customers most likely to respond. Some customers are more likely to respond to incentives, some to differentiated service provided only to loyal customers, while some may only respond to a combination of the two.

Information

> The exchange of information is one of the keys to loyalty, and provides a critical bridge between state of mind and behaviour. Loyal customers are more likely to give information to you (because they trust you and expect you to use it with discretion and to their benefit). They also expect you to be able to access that information during transactions with them. The importance of information technology as the 'corporate memory' of customer information cannot be overstated.

Loyal customers also expect to receive more information from and about you, so 'privileged' communication is an essential element of loyalty programmes.

Customer service implications

Loyal customers often believe they get better service because they are loyal. They feel they are rewarded for their loyalty. This has two implications:

❑ Loyalty approaches should seek to differentiate the relationship and service package provided to loyal customers.
❑ Ways of giving 'special recognition' at the point of customer contact should be used.

Consequences of choice of definition

If the state-of-mind definition of loyalty is used, the focus of the resulting loyalty approach will be on gaining a special place in the mind of the customer, and making the customer feel that their loyalty is being rewarded by stronger or better relationship with you, visible perhaps in a higher level of service. If the behavioural definition is used, the focus of the resulting loyalty approach will be on incentives that reinforce behaviour patterns, illustrated simply in Table 7.3.

Table 7.3 *Consequences of choice of definition*

Definition	Result
State of mind	Managing loyalty is a constant *theme* of the company's approach to managing customers
Behavioural	Loyalty management takes place through one or more *schemes* to reinforce one or more 'loyal' behaviours

But the best approaches apply *both* definitions, just like all good marketing, with any incentives aimed at reinforcing individual loyal behaviours used to draw attention to the benefits of the overall relationship. Let us see how this can be achieved in practice.

MANAGING LOYALTY

If the above view of loyalty is accepted, then managing loyalty becomes much more than devising a promotional scheme to reinforce customers who buy more. Unless a scheme designed to change behaviour reinforces and adds value to the brand, changed behaviour will only last a little longer than the scheme, except where the scheme is used to encourage trial by new users. The petrol retailers were guilty of this with their voucher schemes. Loyalty schemes, by definition, are not of this kind.

Further, managing loyalty means not only managing behaviour but also managing a state of mind. It means affecting the customer's attitude to doing business with the supplier over the long term – not merely until the next visit or the next purchase. This means that a properly managed approach to loyalty must make the customer want to do more business with the supplier over the long term or, at least, sustain their existing level of business.

STEPS IN A LOYALTY-BASED RELATIONSHIP STRATEGY

Customer retention for all customers is key. There are six steps in retention strategy as illustrated in Figure 7.1.

Define objectives

The need to develop a loyalty approach over and above existing marketing, sales, and service approaches should be identified as part of an overall audit of customer management. Such an audit might reveal, for example:

❑ Competitive attempts to target precisely your best customers.
❑ Falling repurchase rate among your best customers.
❑ Falling levels of 'state-of-mind' loyalty.
❑ Increasing rate of customers switching away from your products and services.

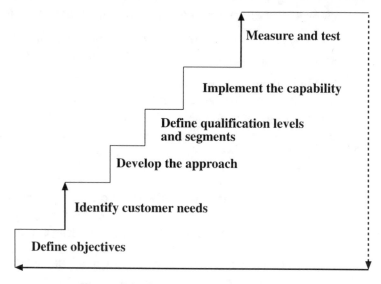

Figure 7.1   Steps in a relationship strategy

Sometimes, the need for a concerted approach to manage loyalty derives from your failure to integrate all elements of the marketing, sales and service mix to focus on customer retention and development. Or it may arise because you identify the opportunity to achieve higher customer-retention performance than the industry standard.

Your objectives for the loyalty approach should be set in quantified terms, or else the approach will be impossible to evaluate, whether by research or through business performance. These objectives should always contain some financial component, or else the loyalty approach may be vulnerable to the criticism that it makes your customers feel good but has no effect on profits.

Adopt the definition of loyalty that makes strategic sense

There are circumstances in which a state-of-mind definition is not feasible. In some markets, commoditisation has taken place, and companies and their products have become undifferentiable (although often this is due to the suppliers' own marketing and service failures). If you are in this position, using incentives to reward specific loyal behaviours may be the only approach that works for you. However, we suggest starting with the state-of-mind definition – perhaps best paraphrased as the *desire* to do business with you and not with your competitors.

Identify your customers' needs (and their propensities to be loyal)

If you are considering introducing a loyalty approach, you must establish, usually through research and/or testing, the following:

❑ Which groups of customers are strategically important to you?
❑ What is the propensity of these groups to respond to different marketing, sales and service approaches?
❑ How, and by how much, do they respond, and in particular, how does their loyalty increase, mentally (as measured by research, perhaps) and behaviourally?

Remember, segmented lifetime value analysis may indicate that smaller, but regular buyers contribute a greater profit margin and lifetime value than single large purchasers.

Your customer base is the greatest potential market-research tool you have. It can provide market researchers with an excellent sampling frame, which is why the formal research process should be built into marketing contacts, involving where possible the use of questionnaires and structured telephone interviews. If executed properly, research will reinforce the brand and values you wish to transmit to customers.

Develop the approach

This involves the following.

Find the best loyalty reinforcers

Identify those aspects of the marketing and service mix which can be deployed most effectively (taking into account the nature of your target customers for the loyalty approach) to reinforce and build loyalty.

There is a tendency to focus first on promotional incentives (discounts, free or low-cost promotional products and services, etc), but these have the disadvantage of focusing on specific behaviours, as the qualification to receive the incentive is usually fixed in terms of those behaviours. A key area of focus should be the interface with the customer. Put simply, how you deal with your customers, in terms of managing their requirements and exchanging information with them, should hold the key to sustaining and building their loyalty.

Find the most valued reinforcers

Find those elements of the product/service mix which have highest perceived value to your customers, but relatively low costs of provision.

This may seem a strange point, but it is the key to most schemes that work in the long term. Financial directors are not keen on giving away profits. The justification of loyalty schemes is that they reduce marketing costs because:

❑ Less has to be spent on acquiring new customers.
❑ It costs less to sell more to existing customers, because we already know them and have access to them.

Loyalty schemes can also reduce service costs, partly because existing customers have learnt how to work with you: hopefully you have taught them! But these financial benefits may take some time to emerge. Meanwhile, the costs of the loyalty approach continue to accumulate.

Here are some good examples of elements which can be built up into good loyalty approaches:

❑ Spare network capacity, eg under-booked flights, weekend and evening phone calls, off-season holidays, day-time/summer electricity.
❑ Services that cost less to provide to loyal customers than when provided on the open market, eg car rescue schemes provided to customers who have their cars serviced according to the manufac-turer's schedule.
❑ Products or services with very high marketing costs (which disappear when they are provided as part of a loyalty approach).
❑ Products or services which customers are prepared to part-pay for (eg points plus cash).
❑ Service 'touches' that cost very little to provide but are different from what your competitors are providing, and have high perceived value, eg special information.

Define qualification levels and segments

This is a detailed analysis of the profile of your best customers. We advise starting with a broad definition of best, rather than just say the top 20 per cent because the next 40 to 50 per cent may offer huge potential. A thorough profiling and tracking of their purchase histories, transactio-nal values, promotional responses, and sources is vital here. It also helps identify the potential market size of similar customers for the acquisition programme. This is sometimes referred to as a relationship marketing audit. Many financial institutions, when they have undertaken this activity, have been surprised to learn how many customers and families are multiple purchasers of the products.

You must work out to which groups of customers you wish to provide the benefits of your loyalty approach, and the divisions between these groups of customers. Conventionally, this is done in terms of how much they buy overall from you, but there are many other approaches (Table 7.4).

Table 7.4 *Different types of segmentation*

Which type of segmentation makes sense for you?

How much they buy of a key product or service
How often they buy
The spread of their purchases
Their potential future purchases
Their actual or potential importance as a recommender of your services
How much you buy from them (for reciprocal approaches)
How much information they give you

It is common to set 'tiered' qualification levels, with increasing loyalty commitment from customers matched by increasing service levels and bonuses from you.

This makes sense provided that the customer's movement between tiers is normally upwards. Being downgraded is not a pleasant experience in any context, but particularly disappointing for customers who have been 'nurtured upwards' for a long period. One demotion can destroy a relationship built up over years. For this reason, the 'slow let-down' must be carefully designed, with early warning and proper explanation, and (in the case of consumer rather than business-to-business approaches) the chance to maintain a higher level of qualification through a subscription fee. Also, it is important not to let temporary reductions in purchasing (which may be totally uncorrelated with loyalty) lead to downgrading. For example, a member of a frequent flyer scheme may temporarily fly less overall, rather than fly more with another airline. Demotivating them by downgrading them immediately makes little sense.

Beware of downgrading customers.

Deliver the capability

Capability is defined as the support infrastructure necessary to 'deliver' relationship marketing. It includes all of the elements described in Chapter 13 and is in some ways the most straightforward part of the process, in the sense that the individual components of the approach are normally a remix or enhancement of existing approaches, using all the well-known tools of marketing and service management. What distinguishes the way they are deployed is the consistency of the approach, which derives from following the above methodology. Integration of all customer contact approaches and the brand mix differentiates customer relationship marketing from other programmes. This consistency and integration should come through in all the key areas, such as:

❑ Briefing marketing service suppliers: advertising and direct marketing agencies, in-house magazine publishers, etc.
❑ Customer service definition.
❑ Staff training and motivation approaches.
❑ Acquisitions, adaptations and development of customer-facing information systems.
❑ Setting pricing and terms of payments.
❑ Policy and process development.

The workload involved in all these is, of course, significant, but the point is that if your approach is developed logically, starting with proper strategic evaluation and with the right analysis of customer needs, behaviour, and experience, then the follow-through should be relatively straightforward, based on a phased approach. Many schemes run into trouble because they are developed in a hurry, to fix a short-term marketing problem, and without regard for the opportunities opened up by a more carefully designed approach.

Measure effectiveness

Loyalty approaches must in the end pay by producing better sales and profits than would have been yielded without the approach. The term 'increase' is avoided here, because sometimes loyalty approaches are required to stem declining sales and profitability.

If you apply the approach to all your best customers, you can't answer the question 'what would have happened to these customers without the loyalty approach?' For this reason, given that the financial director will (and should) ask whether it pays, the opportunity to test the effect of the approach should be taken wherever possible. The best opportunity for this is at the launch of the approach, because it is a contradiction in terms to test a loyalty approach for a short period, and then withdraw it. So consideration should be given to how customers can be divided into relatively 'watertight' compartments, and the approach rolled out slowly, being evaluated, modified, and improved as it is rolled out.

On a more detailed level, whatever stage of the life cycle a customer is at, it is always worth having a continued series of tests to establish optimum timing, frequency, offer, and creative treatments.

RELATIONSHIP PLANNING

To be cost effective, relationship strategies have to be planned in some detail and can result in quite complex programmes.

The purpose of relationship strategy is to maximise an individual's profitable lifetime value as a customer. Active customers can usually easily be identified from records of current transactions. The definition of lapsed and inactive customers varies by the average frequency of transaction in the industry. In merchandise mail order, a lapsed, inactive customer might be defined as one who has not ordered for 12 months, an inactive customer as one who has not ordered for 24 months or more. But for goods with longer re-ordering cycles, these periods might be much longer. If your product is durable and replacement takes place every ten years or so, your customers might consider themselves as loyal to you even if they have not bought for five years. For this reason, companies with long replacement cycle products try to sell lower value items (service, support, parts, etc) on a more regular basis. The main reason for this is to generate revenue, but it also works wonders as a way of keeping in touch with customers.

In general, the longer the known lifetime of a customer or the known *potential* lifetime of a customer, the more promotional activities can be undertaken during the life of the customer with you. At the beginning of the customer's time with you, 'welcome' activities take place. These are followed by promotions encouraging the customer to upgrade or buy additional products or services. Finally, as the end of the product's life with the customer approaches (eg end of subscription, need to replace equipment), renewal activities are initiated. It is worth determining objectives and developing specific programmes for the retention strategies, indicated in Table 7.5.

Table 7.5 *Develop programmes for following retention stages*

Have you defined specific and continuing programmes for the following?	
Welcome cycle	Renewal
Upselling	Lapsed customers
Cross-selling	Inactive customers

Welcome cycle

This is an opportunity to welcome and reassure customers, build loyalty and gain additional customer information. It also opens up the opportunity of providing your customers with initial benefits. Whether a welcome cycle is appropriate will be related to the length of life cycle of the customer.

Upselling

Given a positive reaction to the product/service, a natural next step would be to promote higher-value product/services. In the case of a normal credit card, it could be a privileged customer gold card, in car terms an upmarket model in the range, or in music-product terms a boxed set act to appeal to a buyer of a single CD/cassette album. The appropriate timing of the offer can be determined by previous customer histories. Often this can be achieved by testing and applying the test results using regression analysis to the customer database to give each record an individual score (or likelihood to respond).

Cross-selling

This is a conscious strategy to switch your customers across product categories. For a credit card it could be promoting a home shopping service or wine club. For a car it could be a second car for the family. For a book it could be a music collection.

In both up- and cross-selling, loyal customers should be given some incentive to remain loyal.

Renewal

The length of the renewal cycle should be tested to achieve the optimum results for the minimum expenditure. Inducements to reward loyal customers for their continued patronage are cost effective tactics. Often a renewal cycle will mean a number of timed, relevant, and personal communications before the date of renewal, on the date of renewal, and after the date of renewal. Once the customer has passed the final renewal cycle date, the customer becomes lapsed.

Lapsed customers

Reawakening lapsed customers is usually more cost-effective than recruiting totally new customers, unless they have lapsed because of a fundamental problem in the relationship (eg product quality) or because they have passed out of the target market (eg ageing). There may also be problems with the quality of the information about lapsed customers. However, when data on lapsed customers is available to you, its value can be tested, so the profitability on promotions to lapsed customers does not have to be guessed.

Inactive customers

Here, cost-effectiveness is a more critical issue. These people have not bought or responded to a promotion for longer than lapsed customers. Again, however, the answer is to test and compare the results to the acquisition programme in terms of cost justification.

SUMMARY

Retention (through developing the relationship) is more critical than acquisition as it is usually more cost-effective and profitable. The communications employed in a retention cycle will vary according to the nature of the business, but upgrading or cross-selling can include selective targeting of products, catalogue marketing, telephone upgrading, customer club, questionnaire, and customer care lines.

Make it worthwhile for your customers to stay with you.

The objective of a relationship programme must be to make it worthwhile for your customers to stay with you, which is why a thorough understanding of customer behaviour is vital. There is often a delicate balance between stronger relationship and customer irritation. In any relationship programme, all possible contact points with customers must be reviewed, competitive messages must be taken into account, optimal frequency must be tested, the customers must receive the right products, customer service, and quality. The next chapter shows how you should bring all these activities together.

Chapter 8

Integrating Strategies

CONTACT STRATEGIES AND THE BRAND

It is vital to see customer relationship management not as something which is stand-alone, a separate programme to be developed and operated independently of other business strategies, but as an integral part of the way you do business. Both a long-term dialogue with the customer and the *integration of customer relationship management ideas into branding strategy* are critical to to the success of the approach.

Integrated marketing through a continuous dialogue (the contact strategy)

A good marketing plan will normally contain a number of plans for communicating with customers, each constituting one or more campaign. A campaign consists of a period of structured communication. During a campaign, a customer receives one or more communications, and responds to them. The end result, eg a sale, is achieved. After a time, when all expected responses are in, the campaign is closed.

However, your relationship with customers should not just be a series of unconnected campaigns, interrupted by long periods of silence. You should not just talk to customers when you want to sell them something. This would reduce the chances of your selling to them. It would also ensure that customers are not very satisfied with you.

Your relationship with customers should be a true relationship. In this relationship, you should manage customers to achieve mutual benefit and satisfaction. The campaign is just a tool to focus communications effort. This includes media advertising, direct marketing, public relations, exhibitions and salesforce visits.

Integrated marketing through the brand

Similarly, the elements of the marketing mix are not separate in their effect, but build upon each other. Relationship marketing is delivered through combinations of different elements of the mix and implementation procedures.

The marketing mix must be determined according to your target market. In turn, your approach to market targeting and the marketing mix is determined by your marketing objectives and the conclusions you reach through analysis of your market, as described in this book. Your aim is to combine the mix so as to achieve the desired effect in your target market.

DEVELOPING A CONTACT STRATEGY

Your dialogue with customers must be seen as a continuous series of campaigns, always reinforcing brand values, which are designed to form and develop a relationship. Campaigns aimed at selling particular products and services start with identification or confirmation of customer needs. They end with a series of contacts that yield profit for you and satisfaction for customers. Every distribution and communications channel plays a key role in this. Each channel used in a campaign should move your customers closer to the purchasing decision. Each should also yield information to help you handle customers better.

THE IMPORTANCE OF THE RESPONSE

A contact strategy is not just an outbound 'you contacting the customer' programme. Relationship marketing depends on the collection, maintenance, and regular use of information about customers. In relationship marketing, the response sought, and sometimes unsolicited, from customers at each stage of the relationship varies. It may be a move to the next stage in the sales cycle. Responses sought at different stages include:

❑ Placing an order.
❑ Information enabling qualification of a respondent as a prospect.
❑ Commitment to an appointment with sales staff.
❑ Commitment to attendance at an exhibition, showroom or a sales seminar.

❑ Assurance that a prospect has received all relevant information about a product or service. This enables the sales person to concentrate on selling.

❑ Indication of a favourable disposition to buy.

❑ Acknowledgement of receipt and acceptance of messages that deliver branding information or support.

❑ Allowing an easy channel for a grievance or a minor complaint which, if left to fester, may result in a lost customer.

Customers benefit from a well-planned sales dialogue with you because:

❑ They have the information they need to take decisions.
❑ Their problems may be solved before they occur.
❑ They can make buying decisions with the confidence that they have obtained the right information and developed a good relationship with you, which will ensure that the purchase goes smoothly.

DATA QUALITY

Relationship marketing requires high-quality information about customers. This information may have been collated from various databases: sales order entry, customer service, sales people's files, responses to marketing campaigns, etc.

The database must support tracking of contacts with customers and allow campaign modelling. It should be the *sole* marketing database. It should contain information (provided by *all* marketing and sales groups) about customers, the types of marketing action taken with them and how they have responded. This is critical in managing relationships with customers proactively.

A fully functional, customer-marketing database also allows marketing staff to assess the effectiveness of previous campaigns, and to target future campaigns more accurately.

The more your customer database is used, with customer information and dialogue information being keyed back into the system, the more accurate the data becomes. The more accurate the data, the more able are your sales and marketing teams to address relevant sales and marketing activities to your customers (right time, right offer, right place). If this happens, the more the system will be used. This should result in better, more-lasting business between you and your customers.

If you use several different distribution channels to manage customers, your marketing database may be fed by a variety of operational systems used by different channels to run their daily activities. But the feed must be frequent (ideally on-line or at least overnight processing). A modular approach to operational systems ensures that operational integrity is not compromised by marketing needs.

THE CONTACT STRATEGY

A contact strategy is a particular set of steps used in handling a customer. It starts with the initial contact and goes through to the conclusion of the particular phase in the dialogue, when the customer has either agreed to meet your objective (eg a purchase) or decided not to.

Different contact strategies are used to manage customers through to the sale, eg a letter followed by a telephone call, or a telephone call followed by a sales visit. Contact strategies are formalised, by having well-prepared options to deal with different turns that the dialogue with customers might take, to produce:

❏ Clearer options for customers. For example, not 'do you want more information?' but 'may I send you our brochure?' or 'would you like our salesman to call or to come to our next sales seminar on topic X?'
❏ Economies of scale, eg standard brochure, sales seminar where a dialogue with several customers can be conducted at once.
❏ Control over your next step, eg if there is a standard brochure or regularly scheduled seminars, the process of informing the customer can be handled fairly automatically; if your telemarketing system allows, you can schedule the next call when the customer wants.

THE CAMPAIGN PROCESS

The elements of campaign design are usually summarised as:

❏ Targeting.
❏ Timing.
❏ The offer.
❏ Creative.

'Targeting' relates to whom you contact. Even the best-designed campaign will yield bad results if it is aimed at the wrong customers. 'Timing' relates to when you contact the customer. This can reduce customer satisfaction if it ignores the customer's buying cycles (eg replacement demand, business expansion or move, seasonality, or personal availability, ie freedom to take a call). Targeting and timing, taken together, are 'customer-side' variables. They relate to the ability to identify the market.

The 'offer' is the product or products you are promoting to the customer, together with the packaging of the product and incentives to buy. These elements are combined into an overall offering designed to meet customer needs. Your offer is a critical factor in encouraging the customer to buy. Sending the wrong offer can alienate customers. The 'creative' is how the offer is expressed: the telemarketing script or the copy of the letter and brochure. The offer and the creative, taken together, are 'supplier-side' variables. They relate to your ability to put together the right package for the market.

Campaigns are, in a sense, temporary phenomena. They can conflict with the ideology of a permanent approach to relationship marketing. However, if campaigns are blended together carefully, so that they are seen as a continuing process of finding new ways of meeting customer needs, and caring for customers, they can be a powerful addition to the armoury of relationship marketing. The aim is that each target group of customers or market segment should feel that every communication they receive or make is a natural part of a strengthening relationship.

ENQUIRY MANAGEMENT

The ability to respond to customer needs at the time they are expressed is called *enquiry management*. When customers ask you about a product, their interest in it is usually more than transitory. The interest will not disappear if the response takes time. But the customer may be making similar enquiries of your competitors. If your response is quick and appropriate, you stand a better chance of making the sale.

FULFILMENT

The term fulfilment refers to the process by which the enquiry is managed to the point where the customer is satisfied with the conclusion. Fulfilment may consist of a number of further steps. These include sales visits, telephone calls, invitations to a showroom, sales seminar or exhibition, or an order for the product. There are many different routes an enquiry can take.

TESTING

To get the best response, different approaches are tested. Because relationship marketing techniques allow you to quantify the results of every campaign, testing provides a low-cost way of getting the details of the campaign right and maximising relationship marketing.

TARGETING

The ability to manage your dialogue with customers depends on two kinds of targeting:

❑ *Market targeting*: identifying the kinds of needs which you can satisfy.
❑ *Individual targeting*: selecting individual customers who have these needs.

Good targeting depends on the information on the database being high quality, and on using the right criteria for selecting customers for a campaign. When you use the database to select customers for a campaign, a target customer profile is defined. This indicates the kind of customer you want to attract with the campaign. It gives criteria by which to select customers from the database. Selection is facilitated by the ability to control the target precisely. Controlling selection criteria enables you to test the responses of different types of customer to different approaches. It is vital to observe the segmentation disciplines described in Chapter 5.

MANAGEMENT DISCIPLINES

All relationship marketing activities require tightly controlled, systematic measurement and management. Relationship marketing is often justified by its accountability – you know if a campaign is cost-effective, because all inputs and outputs are measured. It can also be used to match information on marketing performance and on customer needs and satisfaction.

RELATIONSHIP MARKETING AND THE 'BRAND'

The marketing concept that integrates the mix, and makes your relationship with the consumer more coherent, is called *branding*. This is defined as the complete set of values that a prospector customer derives from association with you. These values are created by the operation of the marketing mix on your customer's perceptions. The problem facing most suppliers is that it is not just the *current* marketing mix that matters. Customers have memories. Successful deployment of the marketing mix over a period of years leads to very strong and positive branding.

The brand is therefore an asset which remains valuable even after investment in creating it is reduced. A strong brand can survive weak marketing for a period. However, like any asset, a brand has a tendency to depreciate. This tendency is accelerated if the brand is poorly maintained. Investing in a brand usually requires:

❏ Maintaining the value added by the product range.
❏ Continually reinforcing positive messages through promotion and the contact strategy.

Well-maintained brands have a value that can be measured. Owning a brand gives you the opportunity to make more profit. Creating a brand is one of the best long-term routes to survival and growth. Branding is one of the most effective barriers to entry by new competitors. It is a psychological barrier in consumers' minds that makes them less willing to try other experiences. This barrier also makes them more willing to pay higher prices. A brand strongly associated with good relationship marketing is an excellent barrier to competition.

A strong brand is an excellent barrier to competition.

BRAND VALUES

Branding a product is not a question of developing and emphasising a particular set of product features. Nor is it created by a particular advertising campaign. It is something that exists in customers' minds. Your aim is to get *brand values* associated with your *brand name*. This means that whenever the customer sees or hears your brand name, these values are recalled. When a brand name is strongly established, it makes it much easier for you to get your promotional messages over and makes the contact strategy more effective, because your customers respond to the brand with a positive frame of mind, and become more receptive to further messages.

Branding and the relationship experience

Branding is not created solely, or even principally, by promotion. In many markets, the most powerful weapon is the relationship experience itself.

In fact, if the advertising makes branding claims that are not sustained by the *perceived* experience, it is usually worse than if the claim had never been made. This is because expectations have been raised and then dashed. For example, a bank ran a TV campaign that made relationship claims that were so contrary to its customers' experience that the advertising was stopped mid-way through the campaign! If you want to establish strong branding, you must pay careful attention to *every* aspect of the relationship. That is why *branding* and *contact strategy* have been included in the same chapter in this book.

DETERMINING BRAND VALUES

The brand's values are sustained by the marketing mix. You need to:

❑ Determine what set of values you want your brand to have.
❑ Find out what set of values you actually have.
❑ Make plans to change the actual values to the required set.

Finding out what a brand's values are is done through market research. Usually, customers are given a list of products, services or organisations, and asked what statements come to mind in relation to them. They may be prompted with suggested statements, or asked to suggest their own statements. The list of products, services and suppliers will include close competitors, but also related products and services, and other companies or products whose brand values you might want to emulate or avoid.

You can use the same type of research to establish what sort of values customers would *like* to derive from you. Don't just ask them what they would like to have. This leads to 'wish-lists': long lists of nice things that would be impossible to deliver. It is better to ask what values they are experiencing and enjoying with other products, services, or suppliers. Reports on behaviour, and the reasons for it, are considered a more reliable guide than statements of desires.

Branding is supported by a variety of other concepts. These are discussed below.

POSITIONING

This is an important concept for translating desired brand values into promotional and packaging concepts. It describes how the brand should fit into its competitive market.

In your positioning analysis, you should focus on aspects that consumers say are most important to them. The aim is to determine the positioning customers want and move your product towards it. Positioning is closely related to the *benefits* of the brand, what the customer will get out of buying it.

BRAND PROPOSITION

In the world of advertising, benefits and values are often translated into the brand proposition. These are the *words* that express the values and benefits of the brand most succinctly. This is what you want to occur in customers' minds when they see, hear of, or buy your brand.

BRAND PERSONALITY

This is a term that refers to the embodiment of the brand's values in personal attributes, eg trustworthy, adventurous. It gives advertising agencies a lot of help in determining how you are to be presented.

BRAND COMPETITION

One of the problems facing relationship marketers is how to present the relationship they deliver in a way that stands out from the competition. Customers are subject to so many influences that it is hard to make a real difference stand out. The best way is of course the experience itself, but this assumes that the customer has already bought or experienced the relationship or service. It is hard to steer a course between:

- ❑ A simplistic claim that is just like the one every other supplier is making.
- ❑ A complex claim that lists every feature of relationship and service, and confuses the customer.

BRAND SUPPORT

This refers to the features of the service and the way it is promoted, which support the branding. As was stressed above, the brand must be supported by both the relationship itself and the way it is promoted.

BRANDING OPPORTUNITIES

These are covered in Table 8.1.

Table 8.1   *Customer experience versus brand values*

Do the following customer experiences support your brand values?

Information exchanged during delivery – the type and quality of information given to the customer and by the customer. This may include facts, advice and other help

Environment(s) within which the relationship is delivered

The physical distance between customer and staff, separation by barriers

Amount of time dedicated by the member of staff to each customer

The role and attitudes of each member of staff

Range of relationship options – frequency and type of contact, typical outcomes, etc. Customers generally like to have a choice. You may need to compromise between the large range of choice that customers would like and the small range that can economically be provided

Degree of control by the customer over the relationship

Consistency – whether the relationship meets or exceeds the required standard each time the customer is in contact with the supplier. Note that over-enthusiastic members of staff can be as much of a problem as under-enthusiastic ones, as they may create expectations which cannot be fulfilled next time

Letters, telephone calls, sales visits, posters, inserts – ie all contact media

Timing – how long the contact takes, including waiting time

Cost – how much the customer pays and what other costs are entailed

Availability – of whatever the customer wants

Quality – whether the relationship is as promised

How do you match up? If you had problems relating the checklist points to brand values, think again. There must be a link; all these points are elements of the customer's experience of the brand.

Chapter 9

Channels, Media, and Campaign Planning

Having analysed and segmented your customers, you now need to be able to communicate with them and provide them with appropriate ways of communicating with you. You reach your customers in many ways: retail outlets, electronic media, direct marketing, a calling salesforce, and so on. Most ways of getting to customers require a professional approach to marketing and sales. In this chapter, some of the ways you can use to contact your customers are analysed for their relationship marketing implications.

These ways are:

1. Account management.
2. Selling.
3. Channels of distribution.
4. Channels of communication.
5. Telemarketing.
6. Direct mail.

ACCOUNT MANAGEMENT

This is used when you need to manage complex relationships with your customers, usually with a direct salesforce. Account managers' job descriptions might include the following elements, all of which are of course critical to relationship development, and designed to maximise customer satisfaction, sales and profitability.

❑ Manage the commercial dialogue with the customer and resulting transactions.
❑ Act as the main interface between you and your customers. In many

suppliers, the account manager has principal responsibility for the sales interface, but may work with other sales staff (eg product specialists). The account manager may also have general responsibility for service, support, customer administration (eg invoices) and any other function that comes into direct contact with the customer.

❏ Identify all relevant customer needs (now and in the future). This covers products and services needed, what they are used for, the benefits that are obtained from using them, and so on.

❏ Understand the business situation and organisation of the customer, and how they influence the customer's need for products and services, and ability to pay for them!

❏ Understand the process by which the customer decides to buy relevant products and services (budgeting, decision making, etc).

❏ Become part of the process and act as a consultant to the customer. This includes helping them deal with problems and capture new opportunities through using your products and services.

❏ Present the benefits for the customer of doing business with you.

❏ Identify competitive threats to the supplier's position within the account.

❏ Provide information about the customer to the rest of your organisation.

❏ Provide the customer with information and with a channel for influencing you.

The account manager, whether field or telephone based, must be your representative to the customer, and the customer's representative to you.

A good account management system has the effect of tying the customer and you closely together. It does this by ensuring that both derive great benefit from the relationship.

The depth of the relationship varies with:

❏ *The degree of market maturity.* As your customers learn more about the product or service and how to use it, they may require the services of the account manager less. They develop the ability to act as their own consultants. However, if customer needs, applications, and product or service technologies are evolving fast, the account manager continues to provide a useful service by educating and supporting the customer.

❏ *The type of product or service.* The more essential the product or service is to the customer's own business, the greater the potential for a close relationship, and the greater the desire of the customer for such a relationship.

❑ *The level of potential business in each customer.* If this is very small, you may find it uneconomical to develop a close relationship. However, by using telemarketing and other direct marketing techniques, and carefully planning the contact frequency, you can extend the principle of account management a long way down the market.

❑ *The range of needs to be covered.* Simple needs met by a few products and services do not need deep relationships. Complex needs and great product and service variety do!

The account managing 'type'

Many types of people succeed in account management. Some are very aggressive individuals, who command customers' respect through the ability to manage complex sales, and implement projects authoritatively. Some are the softly-softly type. They are strong on listening skills and expert at getting customers to devise their own solutions, using the supplier's products and services. But not all customers expect the same approach. Nor do all users of the account management approach require the same style. If anything is certain, it is that the really good account manager deploys many skills differently according to the type of customer and selling task, the stage of evolution of the market and customer needs, and the type of product or service.

Skills and abilities

What sort of abilities and skills does the account manager need? Table 9.1 lists those generally felt to be necessary in managing relationships with customers.

It should be clear from this description of the role and skills of the account manager that in situations where a customer is in close contact with you, account management is almost a necessary condition for relationship marketing. Without it, there is high potential for failure to orchestrate the relationship between the customer and the supplier in such a way as to meet customer needs.

SELLING

Selling is an integral part of marketing. Selling is defined as how you:

❑ target individual customers;
❑ identify their needs;
❑ motivate them to buy standard or customised versions of products and

Table 9.1   *Key customer account management skills*

How do you, or your account managers, match up against this list of skills?

Skills of questioning and listening, so as to build up a picture of the customer's needs. Selection of the most relevant information. The ability to visualise the customer's premises, operational area and actual problems is crucial when working solely on the telephone

Analytical skills – the ability to make sense of customer information, and to put it together with information about company products and services to identify opportunities

Product knowledge – not necessarily in technical terms, but in terms that make sense to the customer

The ability to express what you offer (products, support, commitment, etc) in terms of benefits to customers, not just features and functions. Benefits express how a product meets a customer's needs, in the language the customer has used to define these needs. We have to answer the question the customer asks, 'What will it do for me?'

The ability to devise relevant options, so that customers consider they have a real choice, and to match them to different benefits

Negotiating and influencing skills – knowing how to win people's hearts and minds, when to give and when to take, and the ability to handle problems and objections

A steady and strong activity rate, combined with diligence and determination. This does not necessarily mean calling lots of customers, as they may not be good prospects. It does mean working hard and preparing thoroughly, so that every call is an effective one. It also means maintaining a frequency of contact with the customer that the customer perceives to be right. It means determining call objectives and pursuing them thoroughly. However, the smaller the customers are, and the lower their average potential, the higher the calling rate required

Self-management skills – presentation, time management, organisation of information, etc

Consultative skills. These include the ability to see things from the customer's point of view, to identify tasks that need to be done, to recommend how they should be done, and how to use your products and services to ensure that they will be done. This is 'solution selling'. It forms a particularly important part of account defence. Consultative skills are used to show customers how their business problems can be solved by your products and services. Promotional material that customers receive should focus on benefits, not features, and provide account managers with keys to improve their consultative selling performance

The ability to foresee problems that might arise, before or after the sale, and neutralise them

The ability to handle rejection positively

services that have been designed to meet the needs of the market of which they are part.

Marketing cannot succeed without selling, and selling has a hard time without marketing! The sales process is usually described as a multi-stage process. The simplest model is a three-stage one, as follows.

Identifying prospects

Finding out which people or businesses seem most likely to want the products and services. If prospects are not identified, or if your market coverage is weak, the door to competition is opened. However mature your market, you may still need to identify opportunities to turn its customers into customers for its newer products.

Qualifying prospects

Prospects are qualified according to factors such as the intensity of their need, timing of likely purchase, presence of competitive threat, availability of budget, and so on.

Turning prospects into customers

This is achieved by proposing products and services to customers in a form that meets their needs, by giving them real options from which to choose, by negotiating, handling objections, closing the sale, and by managing the process after the sale. These are the real 'sharp-end' sales skills, possession of which quickly sorts out the wheat from the chaff. Although an account manager usually has a defined group of existing customers, it is still critical to identify which of them are good prospects for further development. In other words, even account managers have to go through the full sales cycle.

Just as there is no such thing as a perfect account manager, there is no such thing as a perfect salesperson. The skills required for a good salesperson are similar to those required for account management. Typically, the new business salesman, responsible for opening new accounts, needs to be high on activity and time-management skills. They need the activity rate of a new business salesman combined with the skills of the account manager!

CHANNELS OF DISTRIBUTION

Formally defined, this is the method a company uses to get its products and services to customers and to manage relationships with them before and after the sale.

Channels can be defined *physically*. This covers:

❑ The way a product is transported to a customer, perhaps via a third party.
❑ How the product is stored while it is waiting to be bought.

❏ How the customer comes into physical contact with the supplier.

Channels can also be defined *commercially*. This relates more to the business process at work, and covers:

❏ How customers are identified or how they identify themselves.
❏ How they come into commercial contact with the supplier.
❏ How transactions take place.
❏ How they are completed.
❏ How customers are managed after the sale, and so forth.

Suppliers use different channels of distribution to manage different sizes and types of customers. In some cases, type rather than size of customer may be important. Some companies use channels that are specialised in the needs of particular industry sectors. However, in all cases, the type of channel chosen should be closely supported by the marketing communications policy.

CHANNELS OF COMMUNICATION

These are closely related to a channel of distribution, but not the same. They are a combination of:

❏ The means used to get information about you and your products and services to customers.
❏ The means used to receive information about what customers' needs are, and how customers would like to be dealt with.

The main challenges in communication channel management are listed in Table 9.1. The rest of this chapter provides some pointers for getting channel management right.

Table 9.1 *Key relationship issues in communications*

❏ What mix of communications media to use (eg TV, radio and press advertising, field sales, direct mail, telemarketing, business centres, exhibitions, seminars, etc).
❏ Who you should be communicating with (two-way).
❏ What messages to send via these channels (eg about individual products, or about ranges of products and services that meet identified needs).
❏ How often to send these messages.
❏ What information should be received from customers via these channels.
❏ How to ensure that the different messages do not clash, but are consistent with each other and properly sequenced.

❏ How to coordinate the different channels of communication so as to support distribution channels in their work. Several channels may be used to influence a particular kind of customer, each channel playing a specific role at particular stages in the 'contact strategy'.
❏ How to ensure that your overall brand is properly developed and supported, while promotions for products and services are as effective as possible.
❏ How to do all this cost-effectively.

TELEMARKETING

Telemarketing involves using the telephone as a properly managed part of the marketing, sales, and service mix. It differs from telephone selling, which is aimed at getting sales over the telephone. Teleselling is usually used as a stand-alone strategy rather than an integrated element of the marketing mix. In business-to-business marketing, telemarketing has been used for many years. In consumer marketing, teleselling is still very common, but telemarketing is beginning to be adopted.

Many businesses and consumers find teleselling a nuisance. Consumers have a ready set of excuses to deal with poorly targeted calls. 'I've got one already' or 'we had it done last year' must be the commonest. In business, such calls are often barred by secretaries, acting on their managers' instructions.

Telemarketing is a discipline in the full sense of the word. It involves use of telecommunications equipment and networks by highly trained staff. Their aim is to achieve marketing objectives by carrying out a controlled dialogue with customers who need the benefits provided by the supplier. In so doing, they are supported by systems that allow the company to manage the workflow, measure it, and follow through the outcome of the dialogue.

Telemarketing requires systematic management, measurement, and control of every aspect of its operation. Without this, the relationship between the inputs and outputs of a telemarketing operation will not be known. This information is essential for effectiveness.

Customers find the telephone one of the best ways of conducting their relationship with their suppliers because:

❏ *It saves their time.*They do not have to handle the formality of a sales visit, or travel to see the product.
❏ *It allows them to feel they control the relationship.*They can say when it is convenient to call, and call you when convenient to them. They can terminate the call when they want.
❏ *It gives them information when they need it.*They may find it frustrating to

wait for information to come in the post or during a field sales visit. They can call and you can respond immediately or quite soon after.

❏ *It gives them a direct dialogue with you.*This gives them confidence in the relationship.

Key concepts in telemarketing

A key principle of relationship marketing is the need to be in constant dialogue with customers. This ensures that their needs are being met and that the information on the database is kept fresh. In a dialogue, information flows both ways. This dialogue lasts as long the customer stays with you. It will consist of a series of 'conversations', conducted over the telephone. Letters, brochures, and other material confirm or add to what is said. A sales visit or visit to a showroom takes place where necessary.

Telemarketing in context

Telemarketing helps achieve many objectives. They may be fundamental, 'coal-face' objectives, ie what particular 'customer-facing' staff should do with individual customers. Or they may be higher-level, more strategic objectives. Some examples are listed below.

'*Coal-face' objectives* may include:

❏ Progressing the relationship with the customer;
  – *call handling*: answering customer calls on any matter, whether enquiries about products, requests for service, handling complaints or problems;
  – *moving towards a sale*: lead generation, appointment creation, order taking, seeking or closing, selling up or cross-selling, converting non-sales-related inbound or outbound calls into sales opportunities;
  – *cold calling*: normally as part of a campaign;
  – *building loyalty*: by meeting needs and by just listening and remaining in contact;
❏ Obtaining or providing information;
  – *enquiry screening*: obtaining information to confirm whether a customer is a prospect for a product, or how serious a particular problem is;
  – *customer and market research*: gathering information to use in making business decisions. This includes screening of lists of customers or prospects to be used in particular marketing campaigns;
  – *delivering customised advice.*

More strategic objectives may include:

❏ *Account management.* Improving the quality of account management, so certain groups of customers benefit from a better relationship with you. This may include finding new purchasers within existing accounts, preventing competitive inroads into customers, and reactivating lapsed customers.
❏ *New business.* Identifying and developing new customers and new markets, extending coverage of existing markets, or launching a new product or service.
❏ *Quality.* Improving the effectiveness, professionalism and economics of the salesforce and other channels.

DIRECT MAIL

Direct mail has three main uses:

1. As a prime medium – a self-contained vehicle for selling a product or service, promoting an event, etc.
2. With other media, to support or follow up other activities.
3. As support to a channel – before the sale (eg to provide leads) or after the sale (eg to follow up a sales call).

Targeting

As with all relationship marketing media, targeting is critical. In a mail campaign, unlike telephone marketing and some other media, the response cannot be instantly adjusted at the moment of interaction with the customer. It is no use finding out after the event whether the customer is the right one and whether the form of communication is right for that customer. Though the cost of each communication seems low, the costs of a large campaign are not. Misdirected mailshots waste print and postage and alienate customers. This is one reason why lists based on existing company data are usually the best.

A direct mail campaign requires absolute clarity on what action the customer is expected to take as a result of receiving the communication. The customers' motivation in taking the required step must also be understood. This is one of the prime bases for the design of the mail pack.

The likely response rate and the value of each response are critical in determining how much can be spent on the mail pack.

Components of a mailing

The letter
A letter should accompany any communication you are sending to customers who are in a strong relationship with you. It may help to view the letter in this way.

The outer envelope	The knock on the door
The letter	The sales pitch
The brochure	The product or service demonstration
Samples and testimonials	Reassurance providers
Order form and reply envelope	The close

Just as you would never ask a salesperson simply to show a product without speaking, you should normally never send a brochure without a letter. However, some very successful campaigns have been without letters (or, for that matter, without brochures). There is of course no general rule except that what works, works, and this can only be discovered by testing!

Letters are deceptively simple. Because letters are written often, letter writing is sometimes approached casually. However, the letter has fewer ways of attracting and retaining the reader's attention than other media. But it has a good chance of being read, so effort invested in writing brings rewards. All the rules for writing copy apply to letters, but there are many additional rules for letters which are too detailed to cover here.

The brochure
The brochure complements the letter. If the letter is the salesperson, then the brochure is the product or service demonstration. The brochure should demonstrate the product or service, and turn the letter into pictures. If possible, the product should be shown yielding the benefits claimed for it. It should be supported by a full and logical story, guarantees, and testimonials.

The catalogue
The well-used catalogue indicates a solid relationship with the customer. It is a permanent representative in your customer's office or home, selling all the year round without additional costs of following up. It also supports other channels. It can help your sales staff to sell the full range of products and services without having to explain them all. To achieve this, your catalogue must be a direct response vehicle – more than a listing of product, features, and prices. It must create the desire to buy

and be as readable and productive as any other piece of marketing material. The catalogue can be distributed in various ways: by mail, at exhibitions, handed out by sales staff, at shop counters, and so on.

Order forms

Order forms may be part of a brochure, catalogue or letter, whether separate or detachable. The order form is the salesperson's close, but the salesperson is not there, so you must make it as easy as possible. Typically it should look valuable, be reply paid, with the customer's details already entered and with clear instructions as to how to complete.

The envelope

It is the envelope that encourages the customer to take the step of seeing whether there is useful information contained in it. This usually means overprinting, and using high quality paper.

One-piece mailers

One-piece mailers are being used to reduce costs or to provide ways of giving more material to the customer within a cost budget. They may attract a low response, but this can be made up for by the higher coverage obtained within a given budget.

Enclosures

Many enclosures have been tried, with great success. They include gifts, testimonials, imaginative ways of showing the product in use, samples, guides or other items of enduring value.

Why use direct mail?

The use of direct mail is growing for the same reasons underlying the growth of all direct marketing, namely:

❏ The trend away from mass marketing to more selective marketing, as mass marketing becomes more expensive.
❏ The ability to measure results.
❏ The ability to start and maintain a dialogue with individual customers.
❏ The ability to control costs and risks more accurately, through testing.

The advantages of direct mail are:

❏ It is possible to target highly specifically.
❏ It is personal and confidential.
❏ It is more competitively secret.
❏ The message can be highly specific, enabling you to dovetail it very

closely with messages put out through the less-targeted media, such as television or the national press.

☐ Even in the lowest cost postage bracket, a lot of space is available in which to communicate.
☐ A variety of formats and materials can be used.
☐ There are many opportunities to introduce novelty (eg by different formats and types of enclosure).
☐ Mailings can be scheduled to arrive within a fairly well-defined period.
☐ Testing is relatively easy.
☐ The response vehicle can be defined to ensure that your customers know exactly what to do when they receive the mailing.
☐ Properly planned, it can be much more cost-effective per reply than most other media.

However, direct mail is not a panacea for all needs. Its specific weaknesses are that:

☐ It is not appropriate to all markets. For example, the mail of senior managers of large companies is usually intercepted by secretaries, and any mailings not considered relevant may be rejected.
☐ It is not appropriate to all objectives. For some products, customers may not trust direct mail, preferring to visit a retail outlet to gather information. In this case, it may be appropriate to use direct mail to stimulate customers to visit particular retail outlets.
☐ It cannot be used in isolation to build a brand.
☐ Some customers are very sceptical of direct mail.

The above are limitations that are inherent to the medium. In addition, some weaknesses have arisen because of the way that direct mail is used in practice. These include:

☐ Emphasis on short-term response, rather than relationship building. Now that so many companies are committed to a database marketing approach, this weakness is less obvious than it once was. But there are still many companies who decide to 'do a mailing' to bring in some leads, rent a list, design and dispatch the mailing, and never work out whether the targeting was accurate. All the opportunities for learning and improving are thereby lost, as would be the opportunity to build a customer database.
☐ Tactical rather than strategic. This is related to the above point, but not the same. Even a company with a good customer database could use direct mail entirely tactically, just to generate leads for its

products. Longer-term opportunities for building loyalty, developing a catalogue operation, selling additional products and services, cross-selling, and handling market research might be missed.

The direct mail operation might not be well-integrated with the rest of the company. For example, letters may be going out at the same time that sales or service staff are due to call. Direct mail campaigns may be poorly integrated with the rest of the marketing mix. It may carry conflicting messages.

CAMPAIGN PLANNING

Your relationship marketing contact strategy will require that individual campaigns are targeted at selected customer groups. These campaigns should be planned and run in a similar way to any marketing campaign, with the difference that they are viewed as one element of an integrated approach to the customer and are not designed simply for a one-off sale but for the long-term benefit of the relationship.

Setting campaign objectives

The first step is to determine which marketing objectives can be achieved through your campaign. Table 9.2 lists some types of objective, and the campaigns that might help achieve them.

The objectives form a critical part of the brief to agencies involved in a campaign. If testing forms part of the campaign, or perhaps the whole campaign, the test objectives should be specified clearly.

One rule must always be observed – keep campaign objectives simple and specific. If you want to recruit good new customers, all your objectives should relate to this. Specify what you mean by good customers, how many you want, and by when. Too-complex objectives can lead to a weak campaign.

The information required to justify the campaign is gathered from various sources. These include the salesforce, product or brand managers, market research, distributor sales. Most important of all, if you have a mature database, is your analysis of responses and transactions data on the database.

Table 9.2 *Campaign objectives*

Use this checklist to match against campaigns you have/are about to run

Reinforce brand loyalty

Achieve awareness of the company, of features, advantages and/or benefits of individual products, or of how to buy the product or service

Achieve product positioning

Convey a proposition

Demonstrate benefits

Customer satisfaction, eg draw attention to service benefits

Market defence, eg counter competitive promotion

Attack competition, eg promote to known users of competitive products

Market development, eg turn non-users into users

Get existing users to use more

Re-awaken past customers

Identify new customers among competitive and non-users

Reduce marketing costs

In your planning documentation, which summarises all your campaigns, you must give the justification for the campaign in terms of the main marketing objective that it supports (eg the need to increase sales of a particular product, or to capitalise on a growth trend). The statement should be as specific as possible, particularly in terms of:

❑ The type of customer involved.
❑ The attitudes and behaviour we are trying to influence.
❑ The influence of timing of customer behaviour on timing of campaign (eg when they are most likely to buy).

This provides the key to campaign co-ordination, as well as to setting clear, quantifiable campaign objectives.

RELATIONSHIP OBJECTIVES

Various themes can be developed during a relationship. Here is an example of development of a theme.

Stage 1   Recruit a set of customers (new or existing) into a new
↓   relationship.

Stage 2   Promote to them an offer relevant to the relationship.
↓

Stage 3   Promote second and subsequent offers to them (cross-selling, or
↓   selling one of your products to users of another of your products).

Stage 4   Develop further offers based upon a study of those with the
   ↓   greatest take-up (more cross-selling).
Stage 5   Enrol customers in member-get-member programmes (in
   ↓   which existing customers recruit new customers).
Stage 6   Develop offers that group products together.

The development of a relationship can be over a short period (say six months) or over several years. In practice, very long-term relationships should be composed of a series of short, feasible steps, paid for all along the way by the take-up of offers, and improving in quality as you and your customers both learn more about how to handle the relationship with each other, and you gather more and more information to enable you to do so.

For example, to achieve your objectives you may need to:

❑ Increase usage by existing users.
❑ Get existing customers who don't use your product to start using it.
❑ Make conquest sales from those who do not use it but use competitive products.
❑ Attract totally new customers.

These tasks are arranged in order of difficulty. Earliest results are likely to come from existing customers (they have already demonstrated that they need the product). The slowest results will come from totally new customers. It may be possible to attract a few totally new customers as you begin your campaign sequence, but achieving significant numbers (and getting them to stay with you) is likely to involve a more concerted effort.

Remember, this is the outbound theme of the contact strategy. A relationship is not a one-way monologue from you to the individual. As in a personal relationship, it is about talking, listening, considering and reflecting what you have heard in what you say. You must avoid jumping ahead or assuming the customer's response, but you must also lead the customer. Your theme is needed because it is normally up to you to be the lead partner in the relationship, choosing the subject of discussion.

QUANTIFYING OBJECTIVES

Any objective you set for a campaign should be quantified. What is more, you should also ensure that your campaign plan includes details of how performance against objectives will be measured, whether through responses, actual sales, or research measurements. The proposed quantification should include:

❏ Target levels of achievement.
❏ Dates by which the achievement is to be reached.

For longer-term campaigns, where there is scope for changing the approach during the campaign, interim measures should be considered, to show whether the campaign is achieving its targets, and dates at which these measures are to be taken.

THE IMPORTANCE OF PROCESS

Relationship marketing requires the observance of certain disciplines. The idea behind these is that delivering against objectives requires you to follow certain procedures within particular processes. These are described in the next chapter.

Chapter 10

Process and Procedures

WHAT IS A MANAGEMENT PROCESS?

A management process is simply an organised way of going about things. It requires a clear specification of how different tasks are to be performed. The elements and visible signs of a process are described below.

Formalised planning and decision making

Typically, in a large company, there will be a periodic planning cycle (usually yearly). Decisions will be taken about what is to be done. The tasks, goals and milestones arising will be formally allocated. Once the plan is in force, then progress against it will be reviewed at predetermined intervals, and more often if there are problems!

Information flows

The process for managing operations will be visible in the information flow that take place; between branches and HQ, between different divisions in the HQ, and between staff within branches. These information flows include regular and exception reports on a variety of topics, including those mentioned in Table 10.1.

All this information will normally flow as a result of form filling and computerised data entry at the 'Data capture and/or Generation point' (eg a sales enquiry captured into an inbound telemarketing screen). The Actioning point is the person or department where the data is sent for review and action (eg in our example, the enquiry fulfilment department or agency). Exception reports will normally be required for problem situations and for one-off events, eg non-routine campaigns, new market

Table 10.1 *Identifying information flows*

Identify the major information type/flows impacting on customer relationships	Data capture and/or Generation point	Actioning point	Data passed to
Enquiries received from customers			
Sales material dispatched (eg brochures)			
Credit referrals/application queries			
Orders taken, confirmed and fulfilled			
Payments			
Levels of credit outstanding			
Average price achieved			
Additional purchases made by customers			
Capacity availability and usage			
Use of particular facilities			
Supplies inventory levels			
Customer profiles			
Staff activity productivity			
Profit – by staff group, facility, service type			
Sales/communications campaign results			

research. The 'Data Passed to' column indicates the other people who may be interested in seeing the data (eg sales person responsible for the account; marketing for analysis). Computers reduce the need for form filling and document filing. Staff are thereby allowed to focus more on giving improved service to customers. Indeed, computerisation allows staff to give data to customers more quickly.

Customer databases can be developed so that different people can have access to, and 'view' selected data in the way that makes sense to them and the way they work. Understanding the flow of data at this macro level will help in the development of the IT strategy for customer relationship marketing.

People processes

In large companies, achieving target levels on the items being reported depends on someone having accountability for the achievement of each item. Staff must also be motivated and managed so that they *do* achieve their targets.

For example, if relationship management is an important item, their performance in this respect must be managed properly and then measured.

This means motivating your staff, monitoring their performance, and rewarding them for achieving target levels. The reward does not necessarily have to be financial. It may be through recognition by management or peers, or special benefits. Measurement may be through customer questionnaires, the manager's judgement or feedback from peers.

Defining tasks by time period

In developing processes for relationship marketing, it helps if tasks are divided by the kind of time horizons they involve, eg whether they are daily, weekly, monthly, quarterly, yearly or special.

Daily work is the everyday job of managing individual tasks. Daily work for managers tends to differ from the daily work of non-managerial staff. The work of supervisory staff tends to be a mixture of the two. For management, daily work may include:

❑ Filling forms and data entry.
❑ Filing.
❑ Diary management.
❑ Back-up provision.
❑ People management.
❑ Problem solving.
❑ Meeting management.

At the human level, the focus is on such things as checking that tasks are proceeding properly, managing problems, helping people complete tasks, supporting and giving them lift through motivation.

For non-management staff involved in relationship marketing, the two key daily tasks are:

❑ Managing customers.
❑ Backing up customer management, eg preparation, completing post-contact processing, etc.

The focus here is on individual tasks and the balance between them on a daily basis. As the period of analysis gets longer, management routines start to dominate. Weekly routines tend to relate to issues such as:

❑ Staffing rosters.
❑ Handling typical weekly workload changes (especially between weekday and weekend).
❑ Collating daily results and reporting them.

In capacity-driven businesses, capacity utilisation is likely to be reported and acted upon each week. Weekly meetings with staff for communication, motivation, and performance review are common, particularly in customer-facing work situations. This is because the quality delivered to customers must be constantly managed and monitored.

Monthly and quarterly routines tend to relate to slightly longer-term activities or projects. These are often seasonal. They include:

❑ Putting together plans.
❑ Implementing sales and communication campaigns.
❑ Briefing agencies.
❑ Recruiting, developing, communicating with and motivating staff.
❑ Measuring performance against budget.

Annual routines tend to relate to major activities, and very important projects. These include:

❑ Launching a major new service.
❑ Development and implementation of a strategic communications campaign.
❑ Production of a business-wide plan.

Also included here are longer-term people activities such as:

❑ Appraisal.
❑ Long-term development.
❑ Promotion of key staff.

There is a strong tendency in all businesses for shorter-term tasks to displace the longer-term ones. Planning often gets displaced by the demands of the moment. This may result in your dealing very well with the needs of today and neglecting the needs of tomorrow. For example, existing customers may receive close attention, but nothing is done about recruiting customers for tomorrow.

For this reason, larger companies create strong processes for all their main tasks. Each task is broken down into its elements. Then responsibility is assigned for each element to specific people. Assigning is usually in great detail – what is to be done, by whom, by when, in what form any results are to be presented, how results are to be measured, who is to supervise, and so on.

Defining standards

Once tasks are properly defined and responsibility for their achievement allocated, it is possible to define the standards that apply to the performance of those tasks. This means that tasks must be defined so as to have some measured output.

RUNNING A PROCESS

Some processes can be self-administered. This applies particularly if tasks are simple and routine, and all involved in doing the tasks know exactly:

❑ what the tasks are;
❑ why they are necessary;
❑ the consequences of not doing them.

For example, staff taking bookings know that they have to make certain kinds of checks on availability, and capture certain information on a form. All that staff need to carry out this process successfully is the training, a telephone and the forms. They do not need a checklist or a computer to ensure that they carry out the right steps. However, staff handling complaints over the telephone may need a more formal process, given the immense variety of complaints. Such a process, using checklists, might be necessary to protect the legal position of the company.

Self-administered processes also work well if managers concentrate on managing the exceptions. This should be by strong positive reward for successes *and* for working to the process, and by negative reinforcement for staff not observing agreed processes.

But if tasks are not simple, or required only occasionally, if understanding about the need for them is not widespread, and so on, then a hands-on approach to management may be required. In some cases, a document-intensive process may be used to ensure that people think about what they are doing and communicate it to each other. This is the case, for example, for most planning activities.

MAKING RELATIONSHIP MARKETING WORK THROUGH PROCESSES

If a procedural approach is taken, for it to work, the conditions in Table 10.2 must hold.

Workload planning

The quality of your customer relationship management operations depends critically on proper work design and workload planning. Jobs are built up from detailed task descriptions, which in turn are derived from

Table 10.2   *Process conditions*

Do your key customer relationship processes fulfil the following critieria?

Staff understand the process. This means that they should be trained in the process as part of their normal training programme. This ensures that conformity to the process comes naturally and is not seen as an additional burden.

Roles are allocated clearly, and staff must understand them and have the skills, time and resources to do them – eg what they are accountable for, what they can decide or influence. There are few things more demotivating than being disciplined for not doing something you were not asked or trained to do.

The process produces clear benefits for staff, eg help them work better, reduce tension or conflict, or give them clear standards by which to judge their own performance.

Staff are committed to the process. This must be reinforced by management action (via involvement by management in implementing the process, setting clear priorities, administering rewards and sanctions). Appraisals must take into account contribution to the process.

Management know when someone is or is not carrying out their role, otherwise individual reinforcement cannot take place. A good process ensures that the right information is available at the right time to the right people. This means that the process should produce routine reports that indicate who is succeeding and who is not.

The process is designed to support your marketing objectives and allow staff to work more effectively to achieve it.

---

your (possibly re-engineered) customer relationship management process. Staff performing those tasks have been measured and timed. Staff with less routine jobs have completed time diaries, to allow identification of wasted time or tasks that should be reallocated. Technology has been deployed wherever possible to minimise time not spent managing customers, and to maximise effectiveness and efficiency during customer contact.

Front office and back office

Front-office procedures should primarily serve your customers.

The split between customer-facing (front-office) and company-facing (back-office) tasks must be considered, and systems designed to support each of these functions so that each can concentrate on the task in hand.

Front-office procedures should be designed with the prime objective of serving customers cost-effectively. They must be:

❏ Able to handle variations in the rate at which your customers arrive for processing. If the tasks do not have to be completed while customers are waiting, then a process is required to extract from customers all that is required (information, money, etc) to enable the processing of the case quickly. If the tasks must be completed while the customer is waiting, then processes must also cover how the customer is to be treated while waiting.

❑ Inclusive. They must deal with both your company and customers and the interaction between them. They must also *work* from the point of view of both the company and the customer.

❑ Allow for the different requirements of customers and the different types of customer you have. Types of customer will vary from highly experienced to inexperienced, loyal to 'cherry-picking'.

The reason for the distinction between front office and back office is that it is in the back office where more complex processing of cases takes place. This may include:

❑ Assessment of insurance claims.
❑ Preparing quotations, statements and clarifications.
❑ Reconciling data.

In principle, all these can be done in front of your customers, and many newer companies have all but abolished the back office by using computer systems and processes which enable customer-facing staff to process all but the most complex transactions themselves. But if they can be organised into a 'production' environment, they can be carried out more quickly and reliably than if they are carried out by staff whose attention has to switch between customers and complex case processing. Also, different skills and personalities may be required for the two types of operation. The focus of back-office management should be on cost-effective, speedy and accurate case processing. The focus of front-office management should be on meeting customer needs while staying within cost constraints. Buffers may be required between the two to ensure optimum allocation of effort. These buffers may consist of:

❑ Orderly queuing arrangements for case processing.
❑ Information systems to ensure rapid availability of data on cases on line, in such a way as to prevent back-office staff being disturbed.
❑ Escalation procedures for problem handling.

Where the volume of front-office contact is very high, it can be sorted and centralised into an environment designed to maximise effectiveness, eg a national telephone enquiry service.

PLANNING AND MANAGING TASKS

Attention should be paid to the speed and accuracy with which information gets transferred and processed. Information flowing up from operations should be processed quickly and problems isolated soon after, or even as, they occur. Planning processes should be structured so as to fit the culture of the organisation. If it is centralised, information, decision requirements and accountabilities should be clearly specified. The processes of communication and decision making should be facilitated by the use of standard formats. Diarying of the time of important staff should be closely controlled, and meetings properly managed. Computerised decision-support systems should be used to analyse results and project manage major changes.

This professional approach to day-to-day management is not as common as it should be. The focus is more on immediate results than on improving the way these results are obtained. However, the advent of quality programmes in many companies has brought home the message that it is not possible to divide neatly between how work is carried out and the end result of that work – sales, relationship marketing, etc. So, for example, if customer-handling is not being carried out effectively, then other operating parameters start to deteriorate.

WORK DESIGN

Specify every action required in each task.

Quality programmes have also taught the importance of specifying every action required to achieve particular tasks. In some cases, there will be branching from the main task sequence (eg if the required service or member of staff is not available). The work must then be designed from the point of view of all those involved in the work situation.

If customers are to be cared for, work design must include the customer. For example, at the moment of purchase, the customer will typically be either waiting at a counter or on the end of a telephone line. Anyone who has experienced the frustration of waiting while an inexperienced member of staff consults a complex brochure or an unintelligible computer screen will know what the problems are. The best solution is to simulate the relationship as it is delivered. This will provide all the information needed to optimise the relationship from the customer's point of view. In particular, it is likely to reveal information about how the customer sees the process.

WORK LAYOUT

In many organisations, customers are 'processed' in the manufacturing sense of the term, in that they physically move through the location of service. Too often, the design of these locations maximises back-office space, puts barriers between staff and customers, or causes customers to wait for a long time in uncomfortable situations. The design of environments in which customers are processed are often tested, with staff at their 'workstations', to see whether customer needs are met.

INFORMATION SYSTEMS

As the need for higher productivity, combined with more customer-oriented treatment, has intensified, many organisations have looked to computerisation to cut through this Gordian knot. Once, information systems only carried information on capacity availability, prices and customer debiting. Now, they cover customer histories and customer requirements too. This means that customers and services can be matched more quickly.

PROCESSES AND PROCEDURES: DEFINITIONS

These terms can be defined in many ways. In this book, a *process* is defined as a structured way of handling a series of connected tasks. For example, the process for handling a customer's complaint may involve a set of defined steps, with different options to follow according to the type of complaint and how the customer reacts to each step. A *procedure* determines the detailed actions which should be followed to ensure completion of a task within a process.

Of course, the use of these terms is relative. There may be several layers of process. For example, you may have a planning process within which there are further processes, eg a marketing planning process. A procedure to support a high-level policy might be considered a process seen from the perspective of someone involved in day-to-day operations.

Process analysis

Once relationship marketing strategy has been determined, one of the first steps in ensuring its implementation is to develop a very clear picture of the current processes and procedures in those parts of your company that affect the quality of relationship marketing, and then to determine how these need to be changed to improve quality.

The tool used here is called 'process analysis'. It is nothing more than its name implies: a thorough analysis of all the tasks involved in delivering policy. More detailed analysis can go down to the procedural level.

The first thing that process analysis shows up is how confused the 'real life' situation is. There may be a corporate view on 'how things are done', but this view is unlikely to be sustained by reality. For example, a process may stipulate that certain steps should be followed. Practice may show that these steps are only followed exceptionally, because of the time pressures on the staff concerned. This will indicate the need either to simplify the process (ie less major tasks), to make the procedures for delivering each step in the process more simple (eg less information collected), or to change the objective of the process (eg from minimising refunds to maximising customer loyalty).

RELATIONSHIP MARKETING-ORIENTED PROCESSES

A customer-oriented process is one which has as its main objective the satisfying of customer needs, with a subsidiary requirement being that of checking the 'correctness' of the transaction. An internally oriented process reverses these priorities.

As processes are the main method by which management makes the organisation move, they are critical in determining the quality of customer relationships. If processes are internally oriented, then staff will continually have to fight against these processes to meet customer needs.

FEASIBLE PROCESSES

In some areas areas of policy, commitment to relationship marketing may be more difficult to translate into feasible processes, given the likely variety of your customers' responses to relationship initiatives. Therefore, procedures must be designed to operate quickly as well as fairly. Problems and customer status must be checked quickly. This is why modern information systems and policies that empower front-line staff are required. Also, Plan B procedures are required. These identify in advance the kind of problems that are likely to occur less frequently, and the options available to staff for dealing with them. Plan B procedures must also be designed for the unspecified unexpected! Plan B procedures prevent staff having to break rules or 'get around the system'

Always have a Plan B!

to meet customer requirements. They also save costs, as the optimum way of meeting customer needs is worked out in advance.

SYSTEMS

Irrespective of the degree of centralisation of an organisation, two forces are increasing the needs for systems support to relationship marketing. They are:

❑ The need for higher quality in relationship marketing. Systems are increasingly being used to marshal company resources (including information) to meet customer needs.

❑ The need for greater productivity in relationship marketing – where information systems carry out the job of automating and monitoring work that was done by humans (eg record keeping).

The major development in information systems that relate to relationship marketing are customer information systems, in particular customer database systems. Many large organisations have invested in systems that enable them to call up very quickly details of every customer's relationship with the organisation: sales, service calls, promotions received, etc. However, these systems can be expensive and liable to information overload. Their performance may slow down as they get larger and searches for details of customers take longer. The need to prioritise has become paramount. This means that:

❑ Information about customers should be automated in strict order of priority, measured by the importance of the customers to the organisation. There is little point in having lots of information available about customers with whom the organisation is rarely in contact.

❑ Where particular customers are attached to particular locations (eg if they are managed by a particular sales or service office), it may be better to decentralise the information to these locations. The corporate mainframe keeps updated copies of this information for corporate purposes, eg invoicing, analysis.

❑ The same applies to the kind of information that customers are likely to require from the organisation. There is little point in having lots of information available of the kind that customers rarely need.

❑ The information supplied by the system to policy makers should allow them to identify customer needs, and not just be a record of a few aspects of the relationship between the organisation and its customers.

Additional points are that:

❑ Systems need to be thoroughly tested for the integrity of their data and of their communications links.

❑ Staff operating such systems need to be thoroughly trained before they operate them in front of customers. Very few things are more frustrating than confused operators. The customer immediately suspects that the transaction will fail or be incorrectly recorded.

❑ The integrity and usefulness of systems depends critically on data quality. This has led to a strong emphasis on the part of systems designers on data capture at the point of contact with the customer. This applies to everything from sales transactions, through engineer service calls, to public utility meter reading, telemarketing calls and complaint handling.

INFORMATION SYSTEMS AND PERFORMANCE MEASUREMENT

In many cases, information systems provide the data through which staff are assessed for their success in meeting customer needs. For example, together with sales data, information from customer satisfaction questionnaires may be used to calculate a sales person's bonuses. This carries risks as well as benefits. A significant risk is that, if money depends upon it, staff will try to influence what goes onto the system and, in the worst case, try to alter it. Hence the need for very clear system security provision.

On a more positive note, information systems can make a major contribution to the clarity and speed with which performance measures are made available. The sooner measures are available, and the more clearly they are presented, the quicker action can be taken. Also, computer systems can ensure attributability. They can show which member of staff is most successful in dealing with customers, and which the least.

Too often, when such systems are designed, the emphasis in designing reports is on the needs of middle and senior management. From a relationship marketing perspective, the key need is for your staff dealing with customers and first-line management to have fast, clear reporting – ideally immediately or, at worst, at the end of the working day.

In telemarketing, where much of the data is recorded as part of the normal business process, this frequency of reporting is the norm. The standards of telemarketing can be extended to most areas where there is daily interaction with customers, provided that these requirements are programmed in from the beginning.

PERFORMANCE AND PEOPLE

No matter how good your processes, procedures and systems, in all except the completely automated environment, relationship marketing performance depends upon people – the subject of the next chapter.

Chapter 11
People and Performance

Unless relationship marketing is achieved entirely through automation, it requires getting the right people, motivating and training them well, putting them in the right situation (organisation structure, systems, etc) so that they can manage customers well. Even if the contact with the customer is not face-to-face, but by letter, telephone, or through a machine, people still have an important influence. The organisational structure that they work in will have a profound impact on their ability to deliver the customer relationship policies and processes described in Chapter 10.

EMPOWERING STAFF

Staff who manage customers are usually capable of much more than they are asked to do. That is why policies which empower your staff to manage customers better work so well. It is also why giving the responsibility for improving quality to those who do the work seems to produce the best results. On the other hand, if your staff are not given responsibility commensurate with their ability, their attitude towards customers may become negative. This will be communicated to your customers – usually unconsciously. It is therefore much better to take an optimistic – even aggressive – view of staff's role in dealing with customers.

This is not an argument for radical change in the way you ask your staff to manage customers. People seem to rise best to progressive challenges. Asking staff to find ways to make radical improvements quickly may destabilise them and wreck their confidence. Staff need to learn what works and what does not, by experience. They may also need some training to help them.

If this approach is taken, staff can take on more, and more can be taken on with existing staff. The latter is important, as people cost money.

THE COST OF PEOPLE

In most Western economies, people are getting more expensive. Rising productivity leads to rising real wages, and therefore rising costs of employing people. Added to this, in some countries difficulties in recruiting are being caused by demographic trends, in particular a scarcity of younger people. For these reasons, there is strong pressure to automate and to reserve people for where they really add value to customer management. These trends have been visible in consumer markets for many years, eg in supermarkets. But they have also had a dramatic impact in industrial markets: in such areas as after sales service (where remote diagnostics and service are becoming increasingly common for advanced technical equipment), and field selling (where telephone prospecting and follow-up are being used to reserve the field sales person for the most difficult tasks – such as gathering sensitive information about customer needs and behaviour, and closing complex sales).

In areas of activity where face to face management of customers seems to be indispensable, automation has been introduced to shorten the time it takes to process individual cases. This allows staff to spend more time selling and handling difficult problems.

MANAGING, LEADING, AND EDUCATING CUSTOMERS

The idea that the job of customer-facing staff is just to process cases is not conducive to relationship marketing.

The term 'processing cases' is used in this book to encourage a focus on the 'production' elements of relationship marketing situations. It also recognises the fact that many organisations that serve customers do not see their customers as customers, but see them more as cases. Many public sector bodies (eg courts, benefit and tax offices) are, or were, like this. Also, a fundamental condition of relationship marketing is that cases *do continue* to be processed, but to a higher quality and more to the satisfaction of customers.

Staff are also involved in managing, perhaps leading, and sometimes educating, customers. This is the very opposite of the *'laisser faire'* attitude, which would be characterised by the statement:

I'll meet customers' needs when they come to me, but I won't encourage them to come to me, and when they come I won't tell them what else they can do to get better service.

The opposite approach has these characteristics:

❑ Customers are encouraged to make use of all opportunities to develop better and more profitable relationships with the company.
❑ Customers are led in that direction during every transaction (particularly if unfamiliarity causes them to hold back).
❑ Customers are educated about new relationship standards they can benefit from.

This may seem expensive in the short run, but is vital in the long run, for customer retention.

The facilities that enable staff to provide this enhanced level of service may be provided, but unless staff are trained and motivated to work with customers in this way, you will not derive long-term benefit from it.

STAFF ATTITUDES

In circumstances where productivity and quality underlie the organisation's policies, staff are being given messages that can conflict. Process more cases in the same time, but develop better relationships with them.

Of course, the systems and processes discussed in Chapter 10 provide the solution to the problem – an improved relationship is not inconsistent with less time and cost per case. With the right systems and processes, and in particular clear objectives in handling customers, many companies have shown that automation not only maintains, but improves, relationship marketing. Many customers actually want to be *more* in control of the situation than they have been allowed to in the past. If *they* are controlling the machine, with staff assistance where necessary, the outcome may be better for them.

SIMPLIFICATION OF THE RELATIONSHIP

To allow your customers to be more in control, the relationship may need to be simplified, so that customers can manage it better while not increasing costs by getting it wrong. This can be achieved by standardising what can

happen in each transaction, modularising the relationship, and guiding the customer through each module, with clear information.

MANAGING STAFF WHO MANAGE CUSTOMERS

From the above, it should be clear that staff who manage customers are a special category of staff. To ensure that staff will maximise the relationship marketing opportunity, the rules in Table 11.1 should be followed.

INTERNAL MARKETING

Internal marketing simply applies to your staff all the disciplines of marketing to external customers. The rationale for this is that many staff are internal customers of the policies and processes of relationship marketing.

Internal marketing follows the usual marketing disciplines of:

❏ Understanding the market (in this case what kinds of staff there are, what their needs are, right through to segmentation by factors such as need, attitude, and so on).
❏ Setting objectives (eg in relation to delivery of relationship marketing).
❏ Creating policies (eg to help staff deliver relationship marketing effectively).
❏ Marketing them to staff (using all the required media and communication disciplines).
❏ Measuring results of the marketing, in terms of attitudes and delivered performance.
❏ Improving plans and implementation next time round.

Many ideas that contribute to your ability to deliver relationship marketing have arisen from this approach. When planning an internal marketing programme, the checklist in Table 11.2 may be useful.

MEASURING PERFORMANCE

Performance measurement and staff management are inseparable. If everything is well planned and implemented, the desired customer relationships should be created. But you must be sure that the effect is as intended – hence the need for monitoring, measurement and control.

Performance measurement and staff management are inseparable.

Table 11.1 *Recruiting and managing staff*

Do your policies on customer-facing staff abide by the following rules?

When staff are being recruited, special emphasis should be placed on their openness to attitude change. People with deeply held views about the status of different types of people, or about the roles that they should play, should be avoided.

Training programmes should be constructed so that they provide continuous reinforcement to the objective of managing customer relationships as well as the techniques staff require to do their jobs better. A single blast of relationship ideas at the beginning is not enough. Training programmes should contain a strong role-play element, covering in particular the problematic customer.

Staff should be managed as you wish to manage customers. Here, the rule is 'do as you wish them to'. Organisations that mishandle their staff find it difficult to deliver high standards of relationship management.

Distinguish clearly between the definition of a job on the one hand and the mission or essence of the job on the other hand. It is the latter that should guide staff, not the former. If a job-holder has to step outside the formally defined job to perform the mission (eg managing customers), then this should be encouraged. Management should act as supporters of the mission, not monitors of the job function.

Reward staff for excellent customer management – but in ways that are consistent with the culture. In some cases, congratulations and encouragement may be enough. If financial reward is required, do not make the reward exceptional, as good customer management should be routine. Often, visibility within the organisation (and to customers) is reward enough in itself. However, it is important to ensure that staff who manage customers receive pay that they consider decent, given the norms of the industry.

Where appropriate, help staff create an appearance that is conducive to positive customer attitudes. Provide image wear, or at least set standards of dress. If appearance is important, and one member of staff 'lets the side down', the attitude may be contagious.

Give staff an identity (even a name tag) and a personality, rather than a cipher.

Create the front-line management role as leader, helper, coach and motivator, not just as controller. The latter role is by itself unconducive to relationship marketing.

Ensure that middle managers do not become isolated from customers. Middle managers – one of whose major roles is to provide the connection between plans and implementation – can make or break relationship marketing. If they place too many burdens upon customer-facing staff, and do not see the consequences in terms of relationship marketing, the result may be very destructive. So involve them in all training and communications about relationship marketing. Ensure that their role is defined as much in terms of supporting customer-facing staff as senior management.

Carry out regular audits of staff attitudes, needs and skills, and ensure that they match relationship managament requirements. Make sure that they are detailed and specific, as the customer research should be.

ORGANISATION STRUCTURE

Organisational structure is a complex issue. It is easy to fall into the trap of assuming that decentralisation is somehow a close cousin of relationship marketing. However, this view is superficial. In large companies, at least, many staff apparently quite remote from customers have an influence on the customer relationship. Product planners and even technical researchers or scientists can have an influence, for the

Table 11.2 *Planning an internal marketing programme*

When developing an internal marketing programme, consider the following:

Set clear objectives about what to communicate, and measure the effect of the communication in terms of these original objectives

Cost the communication as an important input into the management process, and set the cost against the measured benefits (to staff and customers)

Identify the difference between the languages of internal and external customers, and match or merge them

Segment the internal audience according to the type of tasks they are required to do and the benefits they derive from doing them, so that the right messages can be sent to the right people (targeting)

Carry out regular staff surveys to measure the effect of internal marketing (and not just to hear the good or bad news about attitudes)

Use a greater variety of media to get messages over, from print, video and multi-media to team briefings (the equivalent of face-to-face contact). The media should be matched against the message complexity, audience type and volume of people to 'inform'

Use professional communications agencies (if the budget can stand it!)

Recognise the importance of creative concepts, compared to pedestrian instructions

Control the frequency and reach of internal communications, so that the right communications are sent out, to the right people at the right time. Otherwise, there is a severe risk of drowning staff in information and exhortation

Recognise the importance of mobilising all staff – wherever they work, as they nearly all have an influence on relationship marketing

extent to which they empathise with customers' needs while planning, creating or designing products will determine whether they produce products which makes it easier for the organisation to care for customers. Information system specifiers and designers can have a dramatic influence on an organisation's ability to manage customers. They can make it easy or hard for staff dealing directly with customers to access information the organisation already holds on customer needs, or to transmit information 'commanding' the organisation to deliver something that meets customer needs.

IS DECENTRALISATION INEVITABLE?

Managing customers does not necessarily require decentralised authority. Rather, it requires *clarity* on the limits of authority at each level and *clear, fast communications* when reference to higher authority is required. It would be nice to say that the optimum situation is complete delegation, but many a good sales person has bankrupted a business in this way! The ideal is therefore clear allocation of accountability in job definitions, while maintaining flexibility to meet customer needs. Of course, provision should also be made for creation of an alternative approach (Plan B) for the occasional unusual customer request.

In the end, the choice between centralisation and decentralisation is less likely to be dictated by relationship marketing requirements than by the culture or style of an organisation. An organisation which has been strongly centralised or decentralised for a number of years is unlikely to be able to switch to the opposite extreme quickly and without cost. The skills required to implement the opposite approach are likely to be scarce.

Which approach is right for you?

This is not easy to answer generally, but there are a few key indicators. From the relationship marketing point of view, centralisation tends to work well when:

❑ There is a high volume of customers in frequent contact with the supplier.
❑ Customers have a well-known set of needs, and these vary little between customers.
❑ The same kinds of transaction or problem tend to recur, and are easy to deal with.
❑ The importance to the customer of each transaction is relatively low.

This does not imply that in these situations, customer management should be entirely centralised. It does imply that policies should be laid down centrally and implemented within tight but simple guidelines.

Decentralisation works well when:

❑ There is a lower volume of customers in contact with you at greatly varying intervals.
❑ Customers' needs vary greatly, and there is little commonality between the needs of different customers.
❑ Transactions and problems vary widely in their nature and significance to customers.
❑ Each transaction is very important to customers.

FUNCTIONAL ISSUES

The second major issue in relation to organisation structure relates not to levels of authority and their location but to functional issues. Once an

rganisation grows beyond a certain size, it generally needs to create a
umber of lines of command to deal with the variety of its activities. Use
Table 11.3 to identify the main approach in your company.

Table 11.3 *Different organisational approaches*

Which approach(es) is followed by your company?

1. *Geographical area*: setting up branches to operate at particular locations or to cover customers
   in particular areas. This approach is most common where demand is widely distributed and
   needs to be dealt with at or near the point of demand.

2. *Customer type*: setting up departments to cover particular types of customer, eg large businesses,
   small businesses and consumers. This is most common where these different types of customer
   have greatly differing needs that cannot be handled by the same kind of people and/or
   processes.

3. *Function or discipline*: setting up departments which carry out specific kinds of tasks, eg
   marketing, finance, production, research and development. This is most common where the
   function requires specific sets of skills and where performance criteria vary greatly between the
   different functions.

4. *Activity or product*: setting up departments responsible for part or all of the process of delivering
   particular products or services to customers, eg in a motor vehicle company, one department for
   commercial vehicles, one for family cars and one for luxury saloons.

In many large organisations these approaches are usually combined. For
example, a large area branch office may be organised by function or
customer type within the office. Combination of approaches usually leads
to an approximation of the matrix organisation structure. In this example,
branch finance staff might report to the branch general manager, but
have a 'dotted line' report into the finance director of the whole
organisation.

The approach may vary according to the stage in the production
process. For example, in a manufacturing company, research and development might be organised by activity or product. Production might be
functionally organised, ie according to the different activities within
production, marketing might be organised by customer type, and distribution by area.

**The reason why these different approaches to organisation
pose problems for relationship marketing is that responsibility for meeting customer needs normally cuts across lines
of organisation. The processes that connect the different
departments will often be designed to meet the needs of
those departments for smooth operation rather than to meet
the needs of customers.**

The more complex your organisation, the more likely it is that its processes and procedures will focus on the smoothness of operation rather than the effects on final customers. For this reason, process analysis must seek to identify each process that has been defined according to this criterion and revise it to ensure that customers' needs come first.

PERFORMANCE INDICATORS AND TARGETS

If you are to measure the effectiveness of the activities of your staff and of your relationship marketing policies, you need to set standards and performance targets. The best – some would say the only – reason for relationship marketing is that it is an investment that pays off. Relationship marketing must be managed, using quantitative data on the extent to which it is being achieved, and on the benefits arising from it. Although precise measurement may not be possible in every situation, it must be attempted. This is because good management depends upon following a simple cycle of plan – implement – monitor – control.

Properly implemented, relationship marketing, productivity, and efficiency, go hand-in-hand. Proper implementation requires including in the scope of relationship marketing projects *all* aspects of the relationship with customers – not just face-to-face treatment, but systems, procedures, products, the management practices of every function, and even strategic plans.

THE FUNDAMENTAL FINANCIAL PREMISE OF RELATIONSHIP MARKETING

The fundamental financial premise of relationship marketing is that any direct costs of relationship marketing can be set against a variety of benefits. These include:

❏ Higher revenue and profit from increased customer retention and more business with retained customers (higher lifetime value). Increasing customer retention can be termed a *revenue defence* benefit.
❏ Revenue from new customers, attracted by the company's reputation (word-of-mouth, promotions or other means) or resulting from (in business-to-business markets) buyers moving between organisations.

❑ Reduced costs of quality (eg handling queries, disaffected customers).

❑ Reduced costs of complexity (as ways of meeting customer needs are found which involve less complex processes and policies).

❑ Reduced direct costs (as customers are allowed to take over those parts of the relationship that they themselves want to do anyway).

❑ Reduced cost of sales (as more expensive channels of communciation with the customer are replaced, at least in part, by less expensive channels).

People performance measures, process performance measures, system performance measures, and in fact any performance measure, should be related, indirectly or directly, to one or more of the benefits on the list above. Measuring against these benefits helps keep a clear focus on *why* something has been set up.

Such benefits take time to pay off. Strictly speaking, you should carry out a Net Present Value calculation to work out whether the action is likely to be worth while. The problem with such evaluations is that they involve forecasting the likely outcome of the change. Although market research can give some indication of the benefits that will arise – in terms of the likelihood of customers remaining loyal or buying more if practices are changed – such intentions data is notoriously suspect. However, if you are committed to relationship marketing, you will be continually making changes, and should therefore develop a sense of the kind of changes in customer behaviour that are likely to result from changes in policy.

TESTING POLICIES

You can test changes in relationship marketing. If you have branches for dealing with customers, or deal with customers mainly through direct marketing techniques (mail, telephone, direct salesforce), you can test an approach on one group of customers. If it works, it can be extended to others. For example, a major airline followed a policy of keeping one group of customers very fully informed of every offer it was promoting, and of a variety of other activities it was engaged in. Another group of customers were given the bare minimum of information. The loyalty and ordering rates of the latter started to fall relative to those of the former. The profit yielded by the additional sales more than outweighed the costs of sending the extra information. In addition, the more informed customers recommended the company more often, so additional benefits might have accrued through word-of-mouth.

TARGET LEVELS OF PERFORMANCE

It is very difficult to predict the returns to the customer, so it is hard to set targets. However, targets based on testing have the dual advantage that they are likely to be more realistic and that staff will *perceive* them as feasible, and therefore make more efforts to surpass them.

Relationship marketing targets are of three basic kinds:

1. Input targets, which measure the work that is *input* into the relationship marketing process, eg more cases processed to quality standards, reductions in queue lengths.
2. Output targets, which measure the results of relationship marketing in terms of what customers do, eg stay loyal, buy more, complain less, say they are more satisfied, write more complimentary letters.
3. Intermediate measures, which relate to what happens to the customer during your processing of their case, eg make contact more frequently to ask for information.

Once these measures have been identified, the relationship between them should be measured.

SETTING STANDARDS

To ensure that operations are delivering as planned, relationship management standards must be set. These should be based on:

❑ Financial targets: these state what must be achieved for efficiency objectives to be achieved.
❑ Relationship delivery targets: as delivered to customers, based on technical measures such as speed of information delivery to customers.
❑ Market performance targets: such as share of the market, your share of the customer's budget, rising sales levels. These are particularly important in a competitive environment.
❑ Customer satisfaction targets: measures of customers' relationship perceptions.

QUANTIFYING STANDARDS

You should quantify all these standards. Do not confuse measurement against targets with research. Research is carried out mainly to find out what policies to implement, or what problems to address. Measurement is undertaken to assess performance in implementing policies. Of course, the two do not separate cleanly. However, the distinction is important because measurement dressed up as research may be incomplete and bring research into disrepute. The golden rule here is not to decide policies until the situation has been researched, and not to measure against until people and systems have been set up to achieve targets, and targets have been agreed and communicated.

Although it should go without saying, it is always worth checking your standards and their associated targets against the checklist in Table 11.4.

Table 11.4   *Relationship management standards*

Are your standards and associated targets . . .

Feasible, in the sense that they relate to areas that staff can in practice control by their actions?

Credible, in that staff believe that they can be achieved, that their measurement can be more or less objective, and that they really do contribute to the well-being of your organisation and its customers?

Focused on your customers and on the policy areas that are most important?

Relevant, ie they must cover the major interfaces between you and your customers, as revealed by the contact audit?

Reliable, ie they must be part of a well-considered and stable policy, which endures, so that staff know that if they help achieve them, they will not be told (now or in the future) that their performance was irrelevant?

Objective, in the sense that it should be absolutely clear when and by how much the situation is improving (or deteriorating)?

Prioritised, in the sense that staff know which are the most important? This is determined by the *mission* of people's jobs

Clearly *beneficial* to the supplier, ie they must contribute to your mission and objectives?

Clearly *beneficial* to customers ie they must help meet customer needs?

Competitive, in the sense that they are set bearing in mind competitive offerings? At least some standards should lead to the creation of a significant difference – a relationship which has clearly describable advantages over that offered by competitors

Progressive, in the sense that they are not fixed but continue moving forward and changing according to changing customer needs?

Presentable, ie they must not be so complicated that staff do not understand what they are or how to achieve them? There is plenty of scope for creative presentation

Try to ensure that most of the data needed for assessing relationship marketing performance arises from the normal information flow rather than from special research. Research is costly and should only be used where its value has been clearly demonstrated. Try to match staff and customers' perceptions and attitudes with financial and market performance. Many relationship marketing problems are picked up first of all in financial figures, then in commercial surveys, and traced back to staff attitudes that are the result of poor management processes. This is a long way round and rather expensive. The ideal is to pick a problem up at its point of origin, eg a change in a process, and not when it has affected financial performance.

KEY PERFORMANCE INDICATORS

The number of indicators that can be used to measure attempts to improve relationship management is very great. However, it is easy not to see the wood for trees. So identify key performance indicators – ones that are so important that achievement of target is well rewarded, and failure to achieve it a cause for immediate remedial action. These indicators should be chosen so they are closely related to your objectives. You must ensure that they are related to what customers view as the key performance criteria.

SETTING TARGETS

Relationship marketing must be underpinned by a clear framework of measurement, which shows whether customers are really being managed well. These measures must be closely related to your overall strategy, and provide a basis for setting targets for individuals and groups (staff and customers). These targets should then be adjusted in the light of experience and, ideally, improving performance. Monitoring of performance against these targets should be a prime input into appraisal of staff and their managers, and should be used to control day-to-day policies.

There are many ways to measure effectiveness. In the end, the most important results are customer satisfaction and brand support, and how these are translated into financial measures, such as revenue and profit.

BUILDING THE VALUE OF CUSTOMERS

Longer-term performance should also be evaluated. This evaluation helps answer questions such as:

❏ Should a particular kind of customer be recruited?
❏ How much should you pay to recruit new customers?
❏ What methods should be used to recruit customers?
❏ How much credit should new customers be given?
❏ What is it worth to the company to reactivate lapsed customers?
❏ Which customers are profitable now, and how profitable are they?

Much statistical experience is built into such models. The more experience you have with your database, the more easily you can develop such a model.

VALUING CUSTOMERS

Customers are expensive to acquire and not easy to keep. If you neglect the acquisition and retention of customers, you will incur high marketing costs relative to any competitors that take more trouble. The marketing information system must therefore give an accurate and up-to-date picture of acquisition and retention. The relevant management report is the *customer inventory*. This shows customer gains and losses, classified in various ways (eg by type of customer, type of product typically bought). If acquiring customers is expensive, why do it? Over the period of a customer's relationship with you, the customer may buy many times, across all your product range. Customer lifetime value measures the net present value of all future contributions to overhead and profit from the customer. It is hard to calculate, but an approximate answer worked out quickly (to a prescribed formula) is far better (and in practice will be almost as accurate!) than a more exact answer calcuated as part of a major consultancy project. If you know:

Customers are expensive to acquire and not easy to keep.

❏ your customer inventory and your recruitment, retention and *attrition rates*;
❏ how much customers in various segments spend with you;
❏ how much it costs to acquire customers of various types;
❏ how much it has cost you to manage the relationship (cost of marketing, sales, service and sometimes distribution);

you have all the information you need to value customers.

If you can compare these figures from before and after the introduction of the customer relationship management concept you can calculate an approximate value of the approach. The motivation for doing this will probably come from a challenge from members of senior management not convinced that the approach adds value. They have every right to challenge where costs are being increased in a business. For this reason, it is always worth taking 'benchmark' figures from your customer database prior to the introduction of relationship marketing so that the:

❑ benefit can be demonstrated against this benchmark;
❑ costs and benefits of relationship enhancement are kept in a true perspective.

Chapter 12

Relationship Marketing and the Customer Database

WHAT AND WHY?

In Chapter 1, we identified the fact that relationship marketing depends on customer information for its effectiveness. Managing the relationship with customers over many contacts, possibly in different locations, would simply be impossible were it not for recent developments in information technology, particularly in the areas of telecommunications and database management.

There is no universally accepted definition of database marketing. Here, the following definition is used.

Database marketing is an interactive approach to marketing, which uses individually addressable marketing media and channels (such as mail, telephone, and the salesforce):

❑ to extend help to a company's target audience;
❑ to stimulate their demand;
❑ to stay close to them by recording and keeping an electronic database memory of customer, prospect and all communication and commercial contacts, to help improve all future contacts and to ensure more realistic planning of all marketing.

HOW IT WORKS

Database marketing starts by creating a bank of information about individual customers (eg taken from orders, enquiries, customer service contacts, research questionnaires, external lists). You use this information to analyse customers buying and enquiry patterns. This, together with the ability the database gives you to contact individual customers through a variety of media, allows you to achieve a number of different objectives, as shown in Table 12.1.

Table 12.1   *The role of the database*

Which of the following objectives does your current database facilitate?

Targeting the design and marketing of products and services more accurately

Promoting the benefits of brand loyalty to customers at risk from competition

Identifying customers most likely to buy new products and services

Increasing sales effectiveness

Supporting low-cost alternatives to traditional sales methods

Making your marketing function more accountable for its results

Improving the link between advertising and sales promotion, product management and sales channels

Improving customer service, by ensuring that all relevant information is available to you at any point in the service relationship

Co-ordinating different aspects of marketing as they affect the individual customer, to achieve full relationship marketing

---

The characteristics of database marketing are listed below:

1. Each actual or potential customer is identified as a record on the marketing database.
2. Each customer record contains information (used to identify likely purchasers of particular products and how they should be approached) on:
   — Identification and access (eg name, address, telephone number)
   — Customer needs and characteristics (demographic and psychographic information about consumers, industry type and decision making unit information for industrial customers)
   — Campaign communications (whether the customer has been exposed to particular marketing communications campaigns)
   — Customer's past responses to communications which form part of the campaigns
   — Past transactions of customers (with your company and possibly with competitors).
3. The information is available to you during each communication with the customer. This enables you to decide on how to respond to the customer's needs.
4. The database is used to record responses of customers to your initiatives (eg marketing communications or sales campaigns).

5. The information is also available to your marketing policy makers. This enables them to decide:

— Which target markets or segments are appropriate for each product or service

— What marketing mix (price, marketing communications, distribution channel, etc) is appropriate for each product in each target market.

6. You use the database to ensure that the approach to the customer is coordinated, and a consistent approach developed. Again, this step is vital in relationship marketing.

7. The database eventually replaces most market research. Marketing campaigns are devised so that the response of customers to the campaign provides information which you are seeking.

The growth of database marketing has been facilitated by:

❏ The powerful processing capability and immense storage capacity of today's computers.

❏ The way telecommunications technology is being harnessed to make customer and market data available to the wide variety of staff involved in your marketing and sales efforts.

THE DATABASE

Information about customers and markets is one of your main assets. The information on a marketing database has to come from somewhere. Database marketing is 'learning by doing', it provides most of the marketing information it needs. Each database marketing action uses information, but it also generates new information. This is because database marketing campaigns ask for responses. Each response contains information, at least it should do. It is up to marketers to make sure that this information is of value.

If your customer responds to an advertisement by calling a toll-free number, the questions the operator asks are designed to:

❏ Qualify the lead for the product or service that is the subject of the campaign.

❏ Provide information that will help in future campaigns.

In this way, database marketing builds up a store of information about individual customers. This information must be held in the most effective way. Unless it can be turned into profit through improved

Don't keep useless information.

relationship marketing and then sales, it is no use. The computer system is crucial for organising the information and making it available.

It must allow your users to:

❑ Analyse and segment the database of buyers and enquirers.
❑ Use high volumes of segmented data for practical use (eg lead generation and qualification, direct order fulfilment, direct mail, telemarketing, assessment of relationship marketing success).

Many customer databases do not do this. They are not designed for marketing. They are more likely to be *operations databases*, used for order processing (order taking, delivery, invoicing, etc) or after-sales service. They record what customers paid, and what they paid for, rather than helping to predict what they might like next!

DATA DESIGN

Computers work best with information that is well organised to start with. That is why database marketing puts a strong emphasis on the structured collection of data. For example, your telemarketing scripts must be designed to get the maximum amount of high quality information possible from customers, in a structured form. This allows the computer to take it without further intervention and add it to its database. The same applies to the design of forms to be completed by customers.

Structured information gathering is essential. Unless this discipline is observed from the beginning, problems will emerge later on. For example, in a business-to-business market, the end of the financial year is significant, either because business customers need to spend pre-allocated budgets, or because they are likely to be tightening their belts.

Database marketing can be put to many uses and applied in many sectors. So there is no general formula stating exactly which data should be included in the database. Each database is tailored to the needs of its users. But it is important to avoid the mistake of designing it on the basis of *past* requirements.

SOURCES OF DATA

A database marketing system normally uses most of the customer information available within your company. However, it organises it differently from the operations databases from which much of this customer information is likely to be drawn. Some new information will come from internal sources, such as your direct salesforce. This *proprietary* data is one of your most valuable assets.

There are two types of data source, internal and external. Internal data include those in Table 12.2.

Table 12.2 *Data types*

Do you capture these internal data types on your database?
Customer files
Order records
Service reports, complaints, etc
Merchandise return records
Salesforce records, technical engineers records
Application forms (eg for credit, insurance, promotional benefits)
Market research
Sales enquiries, general enquires, queries
Warranty cards

External data include compiled and direct response lists from sources outside your company. Also included are classificatory data (eg census data and their derivations), which provide ways of enhancing other external and internal data.

DATA SELECTION

The types of information on the database may include:

❑ Customer or prospect, ie information on how to access customers (eg name, address, telephone number) and on the nature and general behaviour of customers (psychographic and behavioural data).
❑ Transaction, ie information on commercial transactions between you and the customer, eg orders, returns, complaints, service enquiries.
❑ Promotional, ie information on what campaigns (tests and roll outs) have been launched, who has responded to them, what the final results have been in commercial and financial terms.
❑ Product, ie information on which products have been purchased, how often, how much, when last purchased and from where.
❑ Geodemographics, ie information about the areas where customers live and the social or business category they belong to.

The selection of data to include on the database is made according to the revenue stream and feasibility criteria mentioned above. Data should only be included if it helps to answer questions such as those in Table 12.3. If a data item does not help to answer these questions in a way that clearly leads to revenue defence and/or growth, then it should not be included.

Table 12.3   *Reviewing the purpose of holding data*

Does each data element you hold on customers help you answer one or more of these questions?

Who are or will be your customers?

Who in your company is responsible for managing them if anyone (or at least having the responsibility to keep the data up to date)?

What is their purchase potential or how much have they bought from you in the past, how often and when?

How successful have your marketing and sales activities been?

Who buys from which competitors? Can they be switched?

Why do or will they maintain a dialogue with you? How much does this dialogue cost?

How can they be retained?

How can their purchasing from you be increased?

Where can others like them be found?

When are they most receptive to buying from you?

How should they be addressed?

These types of data are considered in more detail below.

Customer data

Many kinds of customer data might be included on the database. Examples for a consumer database include:

First name	Last name
Title	Length of residence in current abode
Salutation	Type of abode and tenure
Name of spouse	Whether recent or anticipated home mover
Address (in meaningful format)	Telephone number
Gender	Special markers (VIP customer, do not promote, shareholder, frequent complainer)
Age	
Income	Responses to questionnaires
Marital status	Geodemographic coding
Number of children	Loyalty index (share of spend)
Names of children	Potential spend index

A business customer database might include:

Company name	Purchasing process
Addresses of head office and relevant sites	Links with other companies
	Revenue and profits – size and growth
Telephone, fax and telex numbers	Type of company (SIC code), number of employees
Account number(s)	Site structure, etc
Names of buyers(s)	Loyalty index (share of spend)
Names of contacts and influencers	Potential spend index

Transaction data

Past transactions are one of the most important indicators of likely future transactions. This means that the transaction data must include information on each customer's past purchasing patterns. So the details of each purchase for each customer must be logged. This includes not only the obvious 'identifying' details (who bought or returned what, when, how, etc), but also the associated marketing data (at what price, from which promotion).

In consumer markets, transaction data can be much more effective as a basis for selection than geodemographic variables in establishing the needs of existing customers in relation to a new product. However, the widespread availability of geodemographic data that are matchable to individual customer data is changing this situation. A consumer products company with limited or no transaction data available can start with a campaign based mainly on geodemographic data. This will normally be organized in a national file based on the electoral roll enhanced with postal coding and possibly telephone numbers. Census information will usually be used to enhance the file further and provide some of the basis for demographic classification. This can create problems of matching addresses to census information. If any internal or research data specific to your market are available to assist in developing a profile of prospective users, this can be used to create a 'scoring module' or 'directory' for selecting target customers from the national file. Similar arguments apply to publicly available databases on business markets.

Product data

In a one-product company, this raises no problem – each transaction is either a sale or a return. If you have a very wide product range, product classification may be problematic, and a numbering system to suit the requirements of database marketing may have to be adopted. Such a system must allow like products to be grouped easily.

Promotion data

Documentation of past and present promotions in some detail (right down to which customers were subject to them, and the media and contact strategy used) is essential if the effectiveness of promotions is to be measured and if promotional planning is to benefit from analysis of the past.

HOLDING THE DATA

Some data must be accessed quickly (eg data on customers who have recently received promotions, been called by a sales person, received a customer service visit). Other data can be accessible with a longer delay, and some might never be entered into the computer database. Care must be taken about which data is kept for quick access, or the system will drown in useless information. So another characteristic of database marketing systems is the constant check kept on which information is useful, and which data are 'nice to know', but not very useful.

Merging external data with proprietary data, or merging data from different proprietary sources, can be a problem. Special computer programs are normally used to do this. Problems arise when an individual or company is listed in different ways in different databases (or even in the same one). If the different databases are combined, customers may be listed more than once. The databases or lists must be 'deduplicated' against each other. Most of this task can be computerised. However, some human intervention may be necessary, as the computer can only deduplicate within certain tolerances. Depending on how important deduplication is, the computer may be asked to list entries where duplicate entry is suspected, for manual correction.

DATA QUALITY

Data does not stay fresh. It becomes stale, as the contact on which it is based recedes into the past. So special exercises are required to check the validity of data and/or update them. Planning for the *maintenance* of the database is the key element of relationship marketing through the database most often ignored by companies.

Plan for the maintenance of the database.

Databases get out of date quickly. People change addresses and jobs. Companies move, job titles change, new companies are set up and companies go out of existence. Errors occur through commission and omission. This is why audits must be undertaken. Questionnaire mailing can be an effective but costly way of improving data quality.

The quality of the data drawn from a database depends mainly on:

❏ how up to date the source data is;
❏ whether it contains the detail needed to access the right individuals (names, addresses, telephone numbers, job titles).

Data quality is measured by the results of the last audit carried out on them. It should be possible to carry out some quality checks via testing.

Each customer or prospect has a history of contact with you. This information is often lost. This has two consequences:

1. You may approach the same customer in successive days (or worse, on the same day) with different messages (or the same message delivered twice). This cannot be avoided – a customer may read an advertisement and receive a mail shot on the same day. But wastefulness can be reduced by ensuring that different direct approaches are co-ordinated.
2. Without a history, you will have no idea where your customer is in the 'buying cycle'. This information is needed to determine when it is appropriate to telephone or schedule a sales visit.

The quality of information therefore also depends on your customer-contact staff (sales, telemarketing, retail branch, etc) understanding the value of high quality information and the importance of their feedback in improving its quality. Every opportunity must be used to improve data quality, during every contact with the customer.

These contacts may be with sales staff, over the telephone, in showrooms and dealer outlets, on service calls, in shops and at exhibitions, by return of guarantees, via competitions and through past customer records. Lists can be traded with relevant businesses. But the advantage of using your own database is that it consists of people who have done and are doing business with you, trust you and therefore respond better to you.

USING THE DATABASE

A true relationship marketing database can be of great value to all marketing and sales staff. Sales staff will use it for contact management and journey planning, marketing staff for marketing planning and analysis. Retail site planners will use it for making site decisions. The database gives a measure of your success in moving a prospect through a sales cycle. This is of great value to sales staff. For example, a list could be produced of customers in a particular market sector with a particular product who have not responded to the last mail shot on the subject. These could either be followed up more forcefully (eg by telephone), or (if there were other priorities) be omitted from a telephone prospecting campaign, because lack of response (perhaps after a second mailing) demonstrated lack of interest.

The history of your relationship with customers can be used to calculate the costs and benefits of acquiring particular kinds of customers, not just for the first sale, but over the life of your relationship with them. Thus, if the database shows that customers who buy product X are 50 per cent more likely to buy product Y than other customers, then the benefits of acquiring a customer for X extend beyond the profit made on X. This enables you to take a more comprehensive view on the viability of particular campaigns.

With a full history of your marketing relationship with customers, the database is used to identify customers most likely to respond positively when you market to them. This is because there is enough information to identify your success in selling to different groups of customers. When a customer is identified as belonging to a particular group, it can usually be assumed that the customer has the same likelihood as other members of the group of buying a particular product. In its most advanced form, this process emerges as 'scoring'. The score given to a customer in relation to a given product is determined by:

❑ analysis of all the customer's characteristics;
❑ assessment as to whether those characteristics, when they appear in whole groups of customers, make those customers likely to buy.

Once the characteristics that are important have been identified, a scoring method can be devised to be applied instantly, by the computer. This score indicates the likelihood that the customer will buy. This information is combined with campaign objectives to determine a priority for the response.

THE INFORMATION SYSTEMS OPPORTUNITY

Relationship marketing depends on the flow of information about the customer and your company, to and from the customer. The continuing advance of IT makes it easier to record customer information, match customers to already recorded information, and attune your offer to the customer. For large companies, information systems become the organisational memory of all recorded contacts. The problem of access to you is removed for customers willing to do it through IT – an increasing proportion of businesses and consumers. This opportunity for improving 'information-driven' relationship marketing is already delivering results for innovative companies who have seen the connection and taken action. In future, we expect relationship marketing to be a constant agenda item for IT management, driven by business strategies premised on information-driven relationship marketing. IT redevelopment can become a major cost area that should be balanced carefully with the benefits.

The growth of the Internet as a provider of standard global access to systems and networks all over the world is an area of huge interest currently, and will very soon become a major consideration for the marketing departments of most large UK organisations marketing to consumers and businesses. It will increasingly be used for one or more of the following:

- ❑ Prospecting.
- ❑ Providing detailed information for customers.
- ❑ Customers providing information to you.
- ❑ Equipment fault finding.
- ❑ Taking applications or orders.
- ❑ Delivering information based product (eg information services, books, magazines, newspapers, video).

THE LEGAL RESPONSIBILITY

The more that you know about a customer, the better you can serve that customer. However, there are limits to information gathering. One limit is the common sense limit of avoiding over-intrusiveness. This is the kind of limit that is best identified in face-to-face transactions. But the law also imposes limitations.

In the UK, in the last decade, regulation of business gave way to de-regulation and freedom to compete. The effects have been seen almost everywhere in the UK economy. For example, the deregulation of the financial services industry has had a significant impact on that industry. Many financial service companies turned to direct marketing as the most cost-effective means of penetrating new markets and launching new products. This led to the accumulation of large amounts of data on individuals. This data was then used to design new products and then to target sales campaigns. Privatisation of the telecommunications industry created a competitor to BT and increased the latter's use of direct marketing as well as making it a more aggressive competitor in the provision of data-related services. BT has one of the largest customer databases in the world.

The liberalisation of media has witnessed the arrival of new terrestrial television channels, cable and satellite channels, and local radio stations. Many of these are now used in conjunction with direct marketing methods, which have the common characteristic that they involve addressing customers individually, whether by post, telephone or through a face-to-face encounter. All these developments have considerably enhanced the opportunities for improving relationship marketing. But at the same time they have increased the risk of error. Large databases are never 100 per cent accurate. The direct marketing industry abounds with tales of poor addressing, the wrong pack being sent to the wrong type of customer, and multiple letters arriving at the same address. Fears have also arisen among consumers about information gathered as the result of one transaction being misused to stimulate another.

Prompted by these developments, there have been major changes in the legislative framework of marketers who use data on individuals. The Data Protection Act 1984 is perhaps the most significant piece of legislation. The requirements of the Act are summarised in Table 12.4.

> The Data Protection Registrar has already issued a number of rulings relating specifically to the use of personal data by the direct marketing industry. Guidance Note 19 (October 1988) requires computerised prospect lists to be compiled and used only with the prior notification (and consent) of data subjects on those lists. A company sending a mailshot to someone who has not given consent to receive it may be subject to criminal prosecution and a large fine. The effect is such as to end third party mailings to names selected from lists of catalogue buyers, unless at the time of data collection the use is foreseen and explained.

A similar approach in Germany had a profound effect on the availability of lists. It reduced 2500 lists five years ago to only 250 lists today. Ironically, companies rent fewer lists, target less well and therefore produce *more* 'junk mail' rather than less!

The German position on data protection contrasts sharply with the US experience. In the United States there are still no federal laws governing data protection although some states do have their own rules. The major

Table 12.4 *Data Protection Act: personal data*

Is the personal data you hold on customers . . .

1. Obtained and processed fairly and lawfully? This means that people who give data should know why they give it and should not be deceived into giving it

2. Held for one or more specified purposes? In other words, it is not legal to collect data without a specified purpose

3. Only disclosed for the purpose held? For example, data collected for the purposes of checking creditworthiness should not be disclosed for the purpose of marketing products. So if the intention is to use it for both, the individual from whom it is being collected should be told so at the time of collection

4. Adequate, relevant and not excessive? In other words, you should be able to justify every element of it in terms of improving your ability to meet customer needs

5. Accurate and updated? It is not enough to collect it and continue to use it, even if it becomes outdated. You should ensure that you budget for this, as it can be very expensive

6. Retained only as long as necessary for the stated purpose or purposes? Provided you use the data as a foundation for building a relationship with customers, this should not pose a problem. But it would be illegal to collect the information, use it once, and then keep it in case it could be sold

7. Accessible to individuals at reasonable intervals and without undue delay or cost? It must also be corrected or erased as appropriate. A charge for access to personal data has been fixed by the Registrar

8. Appropriately secured against unauthorised access, alteration, disclosure or destruction, and against accidental loss or destruction? These are common sense provisions.

---

piece of legislation remains the Privacy Act of 1974. But the Mail Preference Service, which dates from 1971, was lauded in the Privacy Protection Study Commission report. This service has provided consumers with an opportunity to be removed from (or added to) large numbers of mailing lists. Interestingly, three times more people have asked to have their names *added* than have asked to have their names *deleted* from lists!

THE UK MAILING PREFERENCE SERVICE (MPS)

The aim of the MPS is to 'promote with the general public the Direct Marketing Industry in the United Kingdom by providing facilities for the consumer to exercise a choice in regard to the receipt of direct mail'. The emphasis is very much on encouraging the continued growth of direct mail by ensuring that customer alienation is minimised.

With the MPS, consumers may add their name to the register of those not wishing to receive unsolicited direct mail, free of charge. Many add their names in several different formats, according to the formats they are addressed by, so there are many duplicates on the list. The MPS is paid for by the subscribing companies, who include users, agencies, bureaux and list brokers. In order to maintain quality standards, many bureaux and list brokers are insisting that clients lists going into deduplication are MPS-cleaned beforehand.

THE TELEPHONE PREFERENCE SERVICE (TPS)

The aim of the TPS is to do the same as the MPS but for the use of the telephone. This organisation was set up in 1994 and has also published user guidelines for companies involved in telemarketing activities.

FINANCIAL SERVICES ACT

The Financial Services Act 1986 was enacted to provide a fairer framework for the conduct of investment business. The Department of Trade and Industry delegated its regulatory powers to the Securities and Investments Board (SIB), which in turn established the Self Regulatory Organisations (SROs) to police the various branches of the investment industry. For marketers a key clause focuses on polarisation, which requires sellers to be either wholly independent intermediaries selling a range of products or to sell only the products of the parent institution to which they are tied. This requirement has increased the use of alternative channels of distribution, notably direct mail and telemarketing.

The Building Societies Act 1986 gives building societies much more freedom to behave as banks, competing more freely across a wide range of financial services. Again, this has given rise to more direct marketing activity as building societies build databases and cross-sell a wider range of services through different media.

The various privatisations of large state corporations led to massive lists of shareholders being created and then used as a prospecting list for further financial service marketing.

All these developments – and the prospect of more – means that organisations intending to deliver some of their relationship marketing through the use of marketing databases need to be particularly careful to **Observe the law on** observe the law and – just as importantly – the growing number of **data protection.** guidance notes arriving from the Data Protection Registrar.

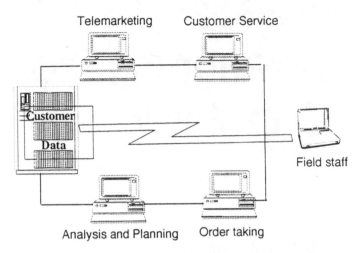

Figure 12.1 Networked data

SUMMARY

This chapter has shown what a customer database is, why it is critical for relationship marketing and the vital legal considerations of holding customer data. This used to be true just of large companies, but with customers' expectations of relationship management increasing all the time, customer databases are being used by even the smallest companies, using stand-alone PC software, which is easy to use. For companies with a few hundred customers, a few products, and infrequent customer contacts, it may be that one personal computer and a database or spreadsheet programme is all that is required.

For larger companies, client-server (see Figure 12.1: the server 'serves' the customer data to the client PCs that use it for various tasks) or mainframe computers that distribute the data across networks may be essential. In some cases, the demands of relationship marketing are so different from the functional demands of transaction managment (sales, service, accounts etc) that the relationship database is kept separate from functional databases, but frequent updating takes place between them.

Pulling it together

This book has developed many ideas on how to establish and improve relationship marketing. In our final chapter, we suggest a process for working through all these issues in your company.

Chapter 13
Developing the Capability

THE TOP DOZEN RULES

This book has given you many ideas about how to improve relationship marketing. In this chapter, we bring them all together. But first, in Table 13.1 we have identified what we believe are the dozen most important rules of relationship marketing. You should identify which of these you don't follow, and what difference it makes to your company.

As we have stated, involving staff and customers in the relationship improvement process is one of the keys to success, and may obviate the need for large research budgets!

THE RELATIONSHIP MARKETER'S JOB

Relationship marketing thrives in a professional marketing atmosphere, one in which it is recognised that the job of marketing is to focus clearly on the six areas in Table 13.2.

In more detail, the steps involved in marketing are:

1. Defining the business that the supplier is in. 'Business definition' is critical. Unless you do this, you will not know which markets to target in step 2, or which customers to care for.
2. Defining and understanding target markets, competition and your own capabilities. This is often called 'environmental analysis', because it deals with the state of affairs in and around a supplier.
3. Setting marketing objectives that are realistic in the light of steps 1 and 2, taking into account the resources at the supplier's disposal.

Table 13.1 *The golden rules of relationship marketing*

The golden rules	Do you do it?	What difference does it make?
1. Determine which groups of customers you wish to serve, and which you don't, taking into account their potential lifetime value to you and their propensity to be loyal or switch. Then identify – using research or feedback – the different relationship requirements of different groups, where appropriate, allowing customers to select themselves into these groups		
2. Recognise that your customers' views of their relationship with you may be very different from yours, and in particular that the customer's perceived transaction period is usually much longer than the actual contact, and that there may well have been several attempted contacts or considered contacts before the actual one		
3. Attune your overall business processes and your customer management processes to customers' relationship requirements		
4. Make it easier for customers to access your company, and then to identify and learn the script for managing a relationship with you		
5. Make it easier for customers to give you information (eg about needs and problems), or ideally, anticipate the information you are likely to need from them and collect it when it suits the customer best, perhaps confirming it when appropriate		
6. Make it easier for customers to extract information and help from your company (eg about how you can help them, the status of their 'case') or ideally, anticipate their need for information and give it to them when it suits them		
7. Educate your customers as to how to get the best from you (the script again)		
8. Help your staff give customers the best service, by an appropriate mix of empowerment of staff, empathy with customers' motivation, information support and the training and development of customer-handling scripts		
9. Let your customers take control when they want, but allow them to give you control when they want to		
10. Treat customers specially who believe they have a special relationship with you (eg because of their loyalty) so that they are not disillusioned		
11. Reduce the error rate in customer transactions – as close to zero as possible		
12. Create a physical or technical environment that makes the customer feel in the right mood/at home doing business with you		

Table 13.2   *Marketing focus*

Which tasks do you relish doing?
1.   Set feasible relationship objectives
2.   Determine strategies to set up the capability to meet these objectives
3.   Put detailed plans together to make these strategies happen
4.   Implement these plans – make it happen
5.   Monitor and control achievement against these plans
6.   Do all this with energy, creativity and flair

4. Determining overall marketing strategies before fine tuning details of policy. The strategies should be based solidly on the analysis under step 2, and aim to achieve what was stated under step 3.
5. Setting out detailed action plans to achieve strategies, remaining faithful to the analysis under step 2. In other words, it is important not to lose sight of the conclusions of the environmental analysis once the stage of detailed action planning is reached.
6. Implementing these action plans professionally, using all the right techniques of general management – in particular communicating with and managing people, managing projects, and keeping tight financial control.
7. Measuring results of actions, and forming conclusions about what worked.
8. Making sure that these conclusions are taken into account in the next marketing plan.

FAILURE IN RELATIONSHIP MARKETING

This logic applies in all marketing situations, and to relationship marketing too. But it often fails to apply. In all sizes of company, there are many factors at work to destroy this nice logical view. These factors are very powerful. Many companies carry out their marketing planning very professionally. But the end result, in terms of what the customer sees and experiences, is not what the supplier thought it had agreed to deliver. Many failures in relationship marketing are caused by the same flaws.

It is sensible to study the factors responsible and to try and anticipate them in your organisation. Forewarned is forearmed! Table 13.3 should help.

Table 13.3   *Failure factors*

Which failure factors are most likely in your organisation?

1. **Unrealistic business definition**. This may be too wide, so that it implies taking on too many competitors with too few resources. Or it may be too narrow, so that it does not take account of developments in closely associated businesses that may end up absorbing or destroying the target market.

2. **Poor information base** – the information on which the plan is based does not reflect realities. For example, information on customers may have come from market research rather than from staff who deal daily with customers, or directly from the customers themselves

3. **Time** – the time taken to plan is too long, so that by the time the plan is to be implemented, it is out of date, and so ignored

4. **Communication** – the plan is not communicated properly to the staff supposed to be implementing it. They do not understand what the plan is, and why they are being asked to do things differently

5. **Motivation** – staff involved in implementing the plan were not involved in producing it, so they do not feel accountability or ownership

6. **Lack of understanding of the relationship marketing concept** by managers trying to implement it (a problem that we hope this book will rectify)

7. **Control** – there is no proper mechanism for measuring whether the plan is being put into practice properly. Typically, all that is being measured is final results, by which time it is too late to do anything

8. **Other priorities** – staff in the field are given too many priorities. Relationship marketing is particularly at risk here if it is perceived to be a luxury (compared to delivering sales, service or product), not essential for the immediate survival of your organisation

9. **Organisation** – related to the above point. If no one's job depends upon making relationship marketing work, then other priorities are likely to dominate

10. **Lack of acceptance** of the concept of relationship marketing. If staff refuse to believe that their jobs hang on your organisation's ability to attract and keep customers, they will never manage customers well

11. **Short-term** emphasis – which produces a focus on short-term profit opportunities and not on real customer needs

12. **Power conflicts** – an unwillingness to give control to or share it with another function or department, despite the fact that this is likely to produce better results for customers

13. **Problems in delivering the plan at the point of contact with the customer**: information systems that cannot handle the requirement, because they were designed to the specification of individual functions, and not for relationship management

14. **Information systems** that can in theory handle the requirement, but prove unwieldy because, for example, they are trying to support too much, eg relationships with every customer rather than the most important customers

15. **Failure to re-engineer business processes** around the concept of customer relationship management, so that relationship marketing policies cause staff to come into conflict with existing processes

16. **The sheer size of your company** and/or the complexity of its relationship with customers (frequency, type, outcomes)

HOW TO AVOID FAILURE

To avoid these problems, you must:

1. Define your business, taking into account what your customers say about what choices they make and what relationship they want with you.
2. Make sure that the information you base your marketing on is as fresh as possible, and comes as directly as possible from the ultimate source – the customer – or from staff who manage them. Information on competitors should come from recent reports.
3. Ensure that information about your customers' relationship needs forms a prime part of the planning process.
4. Do not take too long to plan.
5. Write the plan so that it works as communication and motivation. Follow production of the plan with actions to communicate it, get feedback on it, and motivate your staff.
6. Make sure you get regular progress reports on implementation, not just on final results, and then check the validity of the reports.
7. Measure everything (within reason) that you want to change as a result of relationship marketing, and learn from what you succeeded at or failed to change.
8. Make relationship management part of the accountability of everyone who makes policy about or manages contacts with customers, but also make sure that some people are *totally* accountable for it.
9. Get top management support for relationship marketing.

CAPABILITY DEVELOPMENT

Having warned about the failures and success factors, let's look at the task of developing the capability as illustrated in Figure 3.1 earlier. It is the set of strategies, policies, processes, people and system initiatives designed as individual pieces of a jigsaw, which together deliver the overall aim of managing customer relationships better. Developing a relationship marketing capability is complex because it is all-encompassing, often challenging your traditional ways of doing business. However, as with all complex projects, breaking down the project into individual work areas is the first step. In the checklist starting on page 182 we have attempted to look at all of the work areas that are required. We have added some columns which explain each task in more detail and describe the seniority of the person required to drive the task.

Although as a discipline, relationship marketing if often misunderstood, the techniques we use in developing the capability are well understood. Relationship marketing is different from other forms of marketing only because of the way you *combine* these techniques to produce an organisation with a strong focus on managing relationships with customers throughout your period of contact with them.

MAIN CATEGORIES OF TECHNIQUE

There are six major categories of technique used in developing the capability for relationship marketing, as follows:

1. Strategy development – the development of an overall approach to managing customers. This will be developed from your overall corporate and marketing strategy. This link is important as significant investments and changes in many policy areas, processes and structures are required, in developing your relationship marketing capability, and a link back to corporate strategy may be important to justify the investment to senior management.
2. Customer information strategy – data identification, collection, analysis and interpretation to enable the detailed strategy to be determined with confidence.
3. Planning and internal marketing, which includes:
   — Drawing together all your analyses to produce a case for changing how you manage your customers, plus the associated investment and profit implications, and developing a project plan to manage and monitor.
   — Selling the concept to your own people at all levels within an organisation. The messages and the selling 'levers' to different groups (eg the field salesforce; finance director) will be different.
4. Capability development – the development of the processes, media, systems and organisational infrastructure (organisation, staff recruitment and training etc), to support relationship marketing. This may include longer-term business *culture* change. These together build your capability to deliver the customer management strategy at the point of contact with the customer.
5. Programme development – planning and development of marketing programmes and other tactical activities, which are designed using customer and market data mentioned under step 2, and which use this data to target individual customers, are carried by the media mentioned under step 4, run using the resources and capabilities mentioned under (4) and (5) above, which actually contact customers or invite customers to contact you.

6. The implementation of these programmes in the market, including monitoring and control, and feedback to objectives and strategies.

These tasks or technique areas are all described in detail in the following tables, together with views on who should lead and input to the task, and typical problems or failings. You may not need to do all of these things, and the order of the tasks will depend on many things, but this is the ultimate customer relationship marketing checklist. Good luck!

Technique area	Detailed description, comment and typical problems or failings	Who to lead task?	Team to work on task?
1. Strategy development and analysis	**Developing the overall approach to managing the business**		
Corporate mission, objectives and strategy development	Development of corporate mission, objectives and strategy taking into account the require-ments of customers and your own company's need to build and maintain profitable relationships with customers. This allows other functions, eg operations, finance, personnel, to take these requirements into account when they develop their own functional strategy	Senior management	Senior and middle management
Customer relationship strategy development	Once the corporate level has been dealt with, it is possible to set out your company's strategy for managing customers, in terms of numbers of customers to be recruited and retained, typical volumes and values of business from each customer, how this business is going to be achieved, organisational policy and process changes; through which channels of communication and distribution, etc. This is too often left until marketing strategy development has been completed. A customer relationship strategy is then 'patched' together	Senior manager with RM manager	Middle management, customer-facing personnel, external consultants
Marketing strategy development	This is the marketing functional 'view', in which the acquisition and retention of customers is broken down into the classic elements of the marketing mix – product, price, distribution, marketing communications, etc. It is not advisable to do this in isolation from customer relationship strategy development – the ideal is for the company to develop these two approaches together. The key here is to ensure the sales, marketing and service strategies are developed with the customer relationship strategy as the integrator. This also applies to the rest of the tasks in this section	Senior management (see problems)	Marketing team and RM manager

Sales channel strategy	This determines how your customers would be managed through your sales channels. Sales channels may include: — direct salesforce — third party salesforce — agents — telemarketing/sales operators — retail channel	Senior manager, sales director, taking into account the customer relationship and marketing strategies	Sales managers and RM manager
Customer service strategy	This should include all customer interfacing systems and people, eg billing, service engineers, complaint handlers, technical support	Senior manager, service director	Service team and RM manager
Research relationship needs	A key element of the research must involve best/worst customers and what the customer likes most/dislikes most about the way they are managed by you and/or by the 'best in class' competitors or *comparitors* (companies in parallel industries which are not competitors but their key customer management processes can be compared with yours). The key here is to ensure that the research is *policy* driven	Marketing manager	Marketing, sales, service representatives
Analysis and interpretation	The data available from both customer and competitor research and internal systems must be analysed and the relationship management elements fed into the strategy development	RM manager	Senior manager, marketing personnel, service and sales personnel, external agency
Development of clusters or segments	This takes place at a high level, to help you with strategy development, but may be taken through into a high level of detail if there are large numbers of groups of customers who behave/respond very differently	Marketing manager	RM manager, consultants, marketing analysts
	This allows you to identify prospects with the same characteristics as your (best) existing customers	Marketing manager	RM manager, consultants, marketing analysts
Developing profiling approaches based on segments	This shows the relationship between good customer management and returns to the business, and provides the basis for forecasting. This is required for many purposes, from business case development to planning individual communications	Marketing manager	RM manager, consultants, marketing analysts
Market modelling	Modelling of relationships between customer data, own and competitive policies, and economic, social and demographic data		

2. Customer information strategy and management	Determining all the information you need to build the customer database and manage relationships with customers	Who to lead task?	Team to work on task?
Contact audit	Audit of all points of contact between company and its customers, possible content and outcomes of these contacts, resulting information flows and possible opportunities for enhanced relationship or revenue building	RM manager	Marketing, sales, service representatives
Analysis of content of in-house database	A formal analysis of the marketing database, examining the content, definition, population, age, relevancy, assumed accuracy of the data	RM manager	Systems personnel, marketing representative
Customer data audit – quantity and quality	This will examine the data available within both your systems and relating to the contact audit, data that is currently used in the dialogue between the customer/company, but not captured	RM manager	Systems personnel, marketing representative
Data enhancement	The work carried out above may indicate a need to enhance the data on internal systems. For instance, it may be that some (older) customer groups need to be tested/ researched and may be archived; it may be that some key data fields have appeared incomplete or inaccurate, but still relevant (eg product purchase information, promotion information). Data can be enhanced from internal or external data sources, or from specific research and data gathering exercises	RM manager	Systems personnel, marketing representative
Data strategy development	A strategy for the ongoing maintenance of key data must be developed showing who is responsible, what they have to do, how often and how it will be measured	RM manager	Marketing staff
External data overlays	External data sources including geo- socio- demographic and lifestyle datasets may be researched and obtained to be overlaid on current customer data (eg company finances, credit reference data for consumers) or to potentially add new names to the base	Marketing manager	RM manager, marketing personnel
Other internal sources of data which can be matched back to customers	Examples include responses to earlier promotions, customer service records and surveys	RM manager, then implemented by systems personnel	Systems personnel

Merging of database with those of joint venture partners	This has become increasingly common, as companies identify non-competitive partners with whom they can jointly develop a market. Sometimes, data is pooled with competitors to identify problematic customers (eg in the insurance and credit industries).	Systems manager, once joint venture partners identified by marketing	Systems personnel
Forecasting	Likely evolution of customer base, taking into account attrition and recruitment trends, own policies and likely competitive initiatives	Marketing manager	CRM manager, consultants, marketing analysts

3. Planning and internal marketing	Preparing the company for the move to relationship marketing	Who to lead task?	Team to work on task?
Business case development and project planning	The drawing together of all analyses to produce a case for changing how customers are managed, plus the associated investment and profit implications, and developing a project plan to manage and monitor progress towards improved customer relationship marketing	RM manager	Team from marketing, IT and finance usually
Budgeting worksheet development	Showing how moneys will be spent, what on and what interim benefits will be	RM manager	Team from marketing, IT and finance usually
Lobbying programmes (internal)	Internal lobbying of senior managers for business case sign off is a key task in large organisations.	RM manager	Marketing staff and external consultant
Cultural development, training and education	A key task and in some companies a very long exercise. The key is to plan it as a continuous reinforcement, not as a 'big bang'	Training manager	RM manager and delivery specialists
Paper based, video, electronic or multimedia commun-ication development	The media chosen for internal lobbying needs to be selected according to the message type, complexity, audience size, seniority of personnel and your company's culture	RM manager	Marketing staff, external agencies, training department

Development of prototype 'system' to demonstrate key aspects of the 'new capability/system'	This may help to convince people new to this approach of the systems support required to manage relationships with customers, and to show the difference relationship marketing makes	RM manager	Input from marketing, sales and service staff

4. Capability development	**Putting the infrastructure for relationship management in place**	**Who to lead task?**	**Team to work on task?**
Organisational development and human resource	The relationship marketing strategy may require a very different approach to organisational structure and to recruitment and training	Senior manager, Personnel manager	External consultants, personnel department
Process development	Also called business or customer process re-engineering, this involves recreating the customer management process around the objectives and ideas of relationship marketing	RM manager, supported by IT and personnel management	Other marketing staff, supported by IT and personnel management
Development of systems strategy (eg telemarketing, database, MIS, EPOS, planning etc systems)	Arises from the strategy and data work above. This should be developed from the relationship marketing strategy, and with the customer interface front of mind	Systems manager	RM manager, external consultants, systems analysts
Telemarketing strategy/ telebusiness centre set up	Depending on the RM strategy, this may be necessary and may involve changes in staffing and organisation structure	Senior manager	Sales, marketing, service, systems and external consultant input
Database specification (eg customer, MIS, telemarketing, EPOS, campaign management)	Specification of the systems requirements will emerge from the systems strategy. Note that the system for telemarketing and campaign management may be manual to start with	Systems manager	Business input, external consultants
Pilot database development	A pilot operation for one or two key programmes may help sell the approach	IT manager	RM manager
Application software, evaluation, selection and integration	Software packages may provide the best route to early delivery of all or part of the system solution. Too hasty a choice here can be expensive in the long run, so you must define requirements *very clearly* to ensure correct selection	RM manager	RM manager, IT, marketing and sales personnel, external consultant

Main database development	A very systems intense task, although this may be contracted to a bureau	IT manager	IT, bureaux
Database operation	Given the high volumes of data, some of it not very high quality, this task should be left to skilled professionals	Senior IT manager	IT or bureaux
Monitoring of database activity and data quality	Ensuring that data quality standards are being met. IT people cannot be responsible for data quality. They must monitor it and report anomalies	IT manager	Marketing, and sales managers
Data processing (eg merge, purge, dedupe)	Ensuring that duplicate or incorrect records are deleted or corrected	Marketing manager	Bureaux
Training (customer service, telemarketing, direct marketing)	Ensuring that all staff who interface with customers are trained to handle customers and the systems and processes that have been put into place to help them do so	Training manager	Marketing, sales, service and RM manager
Selecting suppliers (eg agencies, bureaux)	Most companies – particularly those who are new to relationship marketing – require considerable external support. Eventually, they are able to do much more themselves as they learn from their suppliers	RM, advertising, direct marketing and IT managers	Various, external consultants
Change management	The process of moving towards the new way of working needs to be managed properly – at the human and technical level	Senior manager	All functions affected

5. Programme development	Development of particular programmes for managing or contacting customers	Who to lead task?	Team to work on task?
Media planning and use	Nearly all marketing communications media are used in relationship marketing, including direct mail, telephone, and the salesforce, and many different marketing communication disciplines are also involved – eg point of sale, PR, advertising. But the key is to ensure an integrated approach	Advertising and direct marketing management	Agencies
Customer targeting	Detailed analysis of database to identify which groups of customers are appropriate targets for particular initiatives	RM manager	
Campaign planning, co-ordination and scheduling	Campaign objectives, strategies and timings need to be set to maximise effectiveness and minimise overlap	RM manager	All managers responsible for particular media, groups of customers etc.

Test matrix development	Given the cost of communicating with large numbers of customers, campaigns should be tested wherever possible	Direct marketing management	Agencies, external consultants
Creative strategy development	This applies particularly to print and broadcast media, but also to the telephone. It is heavily influenced by the brand	Agencies, marketing director	RM, advertising and direct marketing managers provide feedback

6. Implementation	**Implementing programmes for managing or contacting customers**	**Who to lead task?**	**Team to work on task?**
Project/campaign management of programmes	Checking that campaigns are running to schedule and, if not, chasing	RM manager	Advertising and direct marketing managers
Briefing suppliers (eg agencies, bureaux, mailhouses)	Suppliers need to be properly briefed about their role in each campaign – in time (12 weeks)	Advertising and direct marketing management	RM manager, agencies
Telemarketing script development	Given the high costs of contact, the script must be optimised to get the highest quality, correct information in the shortest time that is consistent with customer service objectives	Direct marketing manager	Telemarketing agency
Actually managing DM campaigns	For example, coding, sending packs out, making calls, handling response	Direct marketing manager	
Lead management	Ensuring that at the point of contact with the customer, the right transactions and information flows are taking place. Lead data out and feedback chased and updated on system	Direct marketing manager	Agencies, customer-facing staff and their managers
Account management of suppliers	Ensuring suppliers' part of the programme is running smoothly, properly communicated to the client, and any problems resolved	Suppliers	
Interpretation and analysis of programmes	Identifying what has worked and not worked and any process/people/policy programmes	RM manager	All marketing management

Note: Implementation is described here in relation to direct marketing campaigns, but similar steps need to be followed for retail compaigns, field sales efforts, etc.

Index